THE NEW
BIOLOGICAL WEAPONS

THE NEW
BIOLOGICAL WEAPONS

Threat, Proliferation, and Control

Malcolm Dando

LYNNE
RIENNER
PUBLISHERS

BOULDER
LONDON

Published in the United States of America in 2001 by
Lynne Rienner Publishers, Inc.
1800 30th Street, Boulder, Colorado 80301
www.rienner.com

and in the United Kingdom by
Lynne Rienner Publishers, Inc.
3 Henrietta Street, Covent Garden, London WC2E 8LU

Library of Congress Cataloging-in-Publication Data
Dando, Malcolm.
   The new biological weapons : threat, proliferation, and control /
by Malcolm Dando.
   p.   cm.
   Includes bibliographical references and index.
   ISBN 1-55587-924-1 (alk. paper)
   1. Biological weapons. 2. Biological arms control. I. Title.
JZ5830.D36   2000
327.1'745—dc21   00-034209

British Cataloguing in Publication Data
A Cataloguing in Publication record for this book
is available from the British Library.

Printed and bound in the United States of America

      The paper used in this publication meets the requirements
 ∞   of the American National Standard for Permanence of
      Paper for Printed Library Materials Z39.48-1984.

   5 4 3 2 1

Contents

Tables & Figures

Acknowledgments

This book was written with the support of the United States Institute of Peace (grant SG-36-98). In previous books I have considered biological agents generally (*Biological Warfare in the 21st Century,* 1994) and incapacitating chemical agents (*A New Form of Warfare,* 1996). Here, I have tried to deal more fully with new (midspectrum) agents that fall between living biological agents and classical chemical agents on the spectrum of chemical and biological threats.

In writing the book I have received much help. I would like to thank both Alistair Hay of the University of Leeds and my colleague Simon Whitby for the use of some of their original source material. I am once again particularly grateful to Julian Perry-Robinson for access to the Harvard-Sussex archive of material on chemical and biological arms and arms control. I have also to thank the Bradford University Life Science librarian Ann Costigan and Mary Pat Wilhelm from the University of Pennsylvania Medical School who replaced her during their academic exchange visits. Both were always willing to assist with my requests for diverse computer database searches and were interested in what I was trying to discover.

My thanks to Mandy Oliver for coming to the rescue in typing drafts during the end game, and most of all to my wife, Janet, for typing most of the manuscript, proofreading, and endless efforts to clarify my meaning. I am of course responsible for any errors that remain.

1

Technological Change and Arms Control

In early 1999 the respected journal *Science* carried an article titled "Terrorism: Defending Against Bugs and Bytes," which reported: "Flanked by Nobel-winner Joshua Lederberg and four cabinet members, President Clinton announced on 22 January at the National Academy of Sciences in Washington, D.C., that he intends to ask Congress for about $2.85 billion to fight terrorist threats to the U.S. civilian population" (1). The article explained that "Clinton said that he has been 'nagging' his staff about bioterrorism 'for the better part of 6 years,' and that Lederberg—a molecular biologist and former president of the Rockefeller University in New York City—helped give credibility to his worries" (1). If Congress approved the expenditure, the funds were to be used for vaccine development, genetic studies of human pathogens, and development of high-speed medical diagnostic systems.

This report was one of many suggesting growing high-level political concern about the possible use of biological weapons (BW)—and not just for terrorist purposes. It has become increasingly evident that ever since the discovery at the end of the nineteenth century that specific microorganisms cause specific diseases in humans, animals, and plants, major states have attempted to develop biological weapons (2). This process began with efforts by both sides (the Central Powers and the Allied Powers) during World War I to damage the valuable draft animal stocks of their enemies. It encompassed the appalling Japanese offensive biological warfare program in China during the 1930s and 1940s, which resulted in many thousands of deaths and the huge and sophisticated British, U.S., and Soviet programs of the mid and later decades of the century.

Consideration of this history leads to the obvious conclusion that biological weapons present a multifaceted threat. We should not just be concerned about the use of such weapons for bioterrorism, assassination, or economic warfare against staple crops, but also for tactical or strategic military use on the battlefield and as weapons of mass destruction equivalent in potential lethality to nuclear weapons. Moreover, the different types of weapons agents—bacteria, viruses, toxins, bioregulators—can each cause widely varying disease syndromes that require detection and recognition prior to treatment (3).

Nuclear weapons are subject to the relatively robust Nuclear Non-Proliferation Treaty (NPT) regime, and chemical weapons (CW) to the strong, recently agreed Chemical Weapons Convention (CWC). But most biological weapons are controlled only by the 1972 Biological and Toxin Weapons Convention (BTWC), which currently lacks any effective verification mechanism. (There is, however, some overlap between the CWC and the BTWC in that inert chemicals of biological origin such as toxins fall under both conventions.) As will become evident, biological weapons pose a rapidly evolving threat because of the current revolution in biotechnology that is epitomized by the Human Genome Project (HGP) (4). Therefore, political anxieties about biological weapons cannot and must not be lightly dismissed. This book is concerned with the threat that some of these weapons pose, with their proliferation, and with how they can best be controlled. It begins with an overview of the current capabilities for arms control.

THE NECESSITY OF ARMS CONTROL

In the early 1990s, during the euphoria that accompanied the ending of the long East-West Cold War, there was a brief period when it seemed to many that the need for arms control and disarmament agreements was over. The process initiated at the Stockholm Conference on Confidence and Security-Building Measures in 1986 had led to the agreement on the Intermediate Nuclear Forces (INF) Treaty between the United States and the Soviet Union in 1987, and the thirty-nation multilateral Treaty on Conventional Forces in Europe in 1990. The vast stocks of armaments built up during the military confrontation that had existed since World War II appeared to be melting away.

There have always been differing views on the utility of arms control (5). Extreme realists, who believe that a balance of power is the best basis for deterrence in an anarchic world of competing states, see little value in arms control at any time. What happened at the end of the Cold War, however, was that even those who saw some value in arms control in a semi-anarchic world (of partly competing and partly cooperating states) wondered about its continuing relevance. Lawrence Freedman, professor of War Studies at Kings College, London, put the point eloquently at that time: "Yet there is a particular poignancy here for arms control in that on the eve of its greatest triumph its relevance is widely questioned and the political events which made rapid progress possible have now moved so fast as to whisk the triumph away from its grasp" (6). In short, if we had moved into a peaceful cooperative world system, what need was there for arms control?

Looking back to the late 1990s, when the Indian and Pakistani nuclear weapons tests brought the whole nonproliferation regime into question, that initial post–Cold War euphoria seems misplaced (7). Many scholars have attempted to reformulate ideas on arms control in light of the new situation after the Cold War. In 1992, in one of the earliest attempts, Ivo Daalder suggested that it was useful to think of political relations between states ranging along a continuum from all-out war to peaceful cooperation. Between these two points arms control might serve two functions; first, in what might be termed traditional *competitive arms control,* to prevent movement toward warfare; and second, to help transform relations toward a more peaceful state, in what could be called *cooperative arms control* (8). Although the international state system has been in a transitional phase since the Cold War, it is clear that there will be a continuing need for arms control, both to moderate the worst excesses of competition and to help movements toward positive cooperation among states (9).

THE NATURE OF ARMS CONTROL

Most people's understanding of arms control today dates from the early 1960s, when a particular formulation was developed in the United States to deal with the problems considered to be important during the Cold War: "preserving a stigma against nuclear use through maintenance of a high threshold between conventional and nuclear weapons; the creation and preservation of redundant and survivable strategic nuclear systems in the Soviet Union and the United States; and prevention of the spread of nuclear weapons to other states" (10).

Arms control, in this formulation, is primarily a bilateral exercise between two superpowers concentrated on nuclear systems and concerned with arms race and crisis stability. From this conception flowed the classic Cold War agreements: the Hot Line Agreement of 1963; the Partial Test Ban Treaty (PTBT) of 1963; the Nuclear Non-Proliferation Treaty of 1968; the Interim Agreement on Limitation of Strategic Offensive Arms (SALT I) of 1972; and the Treaty on the Limitation of Anti-Ballistic Missile Systems (ABM) of 1972.

Despite efforts at reformulating arms control since the Cold War, this conception is still powerful in the minds of many in the strategic studies community. As Gregory Rattray argued in his introduction to *Arms Control:*

Toward the 21st Century, "The central theme of this is that *while the ne-gotiating methods, regions of concern, and weapons involved may be changing, the underlying principles and objectives of arms control remain relevant in the post–Cold War world*" (original emphasis) (11). The con-tributors to that volume agreed to define arms control as "*a process in-volving specific, declared steps by a state to enhance security through co-operation with other states.* These steps can be unilateral, bilateral, or multilateral. Cooperation can be implicit as well as explicit" (original em-phasis) (11). This is no doubt a definition that encompasses much more than the generation of formal arms control treaties. It could involve, for example, unilateral arms reductions without explicit agreement of recip-rocal actions by others.

Rattray, however, does not accept the objective of complete disarma-ment: "The goal of complete disarmament, nuclear and otherwise, may ap-pear desirable at first glance. However, the apparent barriers to achieving such a goal and its possible consequences require us to examine less radi-cal, though still important, steps to improve our national security through arms control" (11). On the other hand, while rejecting complete disarma-ment, he does not accept the objective of coercive arms control either: "Another common motive is to disarm perceived aggressors—as was done with Germany after World War I, Germany and Japan after World War II, and Iraq after the Gulf War. . . . This type of action falls outside . . . the definition that we outline for this text" (11). Although this "topping and tailing" of arms control—leaving it as an expanded version of the Cold War conception—has the advantage of giving a clarity to the definition of arms control, it seems too narrow for our purposes here because it could exclude measures that others view as part of arms control.

Nancy Gallagher, in the introduction to a book of essays that explicitly sets out to encompass a wide range of viewpoints, defined arms control broadly to encompass any type of cooperative measure meant to reduce the costs and risks associated with the acquisition, threat, and use of military force (5). This would appear to accept disarmament but reject coercive arms control.

Such differences are common in definitions of arms control today, as Jozef Goldblat notes in his classic text *Arms Control: A Guide to Negotia-tions and Agreements:* "Today, the term 'arms control' is often used inter-changeably with 'arms regulation,' 'arms limitation' and even 'disarma-ment'" (12). Goldblat suggests that arms control has come to include a wide range of measures intended to "(a) freeze, limit, reduce or abolish certain categories of weapons; (b) prevent certain military activities; (c) regulate the deployment of armed forces; [and] (d) proscribe transfers of some militarily important items" (12). The measures are additionally in-tended to "(e) reduce the risk of accidental war; (f) constrain or prohibit the use of certain weapons or methods of war; and (g) build up confidence among states through greater openness in military matters" (12). However, though his inclusive definitions can cover some specific processes of disarmament, he believes there are limits to what can be achieved in the present world order. He argues that "[e]stablishing very low levels of armaments, not to mention worldwide disarmament, would call for a new world order, one which would permit nations to diminish their reliance on national forces, if not to forego altogether the prerogative of providing for their own defence" (12). This reflects the widespread view in the security community that while armaments can exacerbate conflicts, there are many other—and deeper—causes of warfare.

Warfare may not be a necessarily inherent characteristic of human society in the future, but it has certainly been an endemic feature of the modern state system and is likely to remain so for some time to come (13). Though our understanding of the causes of warfare remains limited, political entities have long recognized the advantages of arms regulation (14). Stuart Croft has argued, in his innovative history and typology of arms control, that although arms control is usually seen as a modern invention, it has, in fact, a very long history. In his view, "[a]rms control agreements can be identified not only in the inter-war period of the twentieth century, but also in the eighteenth and nineteenth centuries, in the Middle Ages, and even in the ancient world" (15). Croft includes in his definition of arms control "not only traditional arms control agreements . . . but also agreements over the forcible disarmament of groups and states by international bodies . . . and agreements concerning the behaviour of states." It is this very broad view of the nature of arms control that is adopted here.

Croft argues, essentially, that over time political entities have developed a set of tools (political instruments) to deal with problems related to military forces. From this very broad viewpoint, at the end of the Cold War period it was possible to see that five main types of arms control were available for dealing with current problems: "(1) arms control at the conclusions of conflicts; (2) arms control to further strategic stability; (3) arms control to create norms of behaviour; (4) arms control to manage the proliferation of weapons; and (5) arms control by international organisation" (15). So what was understood as arms control during the Cold War— bilateral agreements to try to strengthen strategic nuclear stability—was but one subset of one aspect of the whole of arms control.

Examined from this viewpoint, type 2 arms control in the list above does not just include SALT I and the ABM Treaty of the post–World War II years but the Washington Naval Treaty of 1922 between the United States, Great Britain, France, Italy, and Japan, and the update in the London Naval Treaties of 1930 and 1936, as well as the 1930 agreement between Turkey and Greece, the 1931 agreement between Turkey and the Soviet Union, and so on. Type 1 arms control does not just include the United Nations Security Council actions against Iraq following the 1991 conflict but the demilitarization of Germany following both World Wars. It also includes the Treaty of Utrecht of 1713 in which the French agreed to British demands for the fortifications of Dunkirk to be razed, and the unequal treaty imposed by Rome on Carthage in 201 B.C. Croft argues, similarly, that a number of attempts were made to create norms of behavior in arms control (type 3): the Geneva Protocol of 1925, prohibiting the use of chemical and biological weapons; the Geneva Conventions, developed first in 1864, revised in 1906, 1929, 1949, and added to in 1977; The Hague Conventions of 1899 and 1907; and the Peace of God in the Synod of Charoux in 989. Arms control to manage proliferation (type 4) would include not only the NPT but all the efforts following World War I to regulate the spread of conventional weaponry. Finally, it should be remembered that massive efforts were made during the 1920s and 1930s to achieve various forms of arms regulation within the League of Nations system. Indeed, arms control by international organization (type 5) was probably more central to the League of Nations than it was to the United Nations for much of its first fifty years. In summary, then, we might consider that one way of thinking about the regulation of armaments is in the following categories and subcategories:

General and complete disarmament
Arms control
  cooperative (informal unilateral initiatives)
  cooperative/competitive (formal arms control agreements)
  coercive (war termination arrangements)

The main concern here is with the formal arms control agreements reached by partly competing, partly cooperating states. However, we cannot ignore informal cooperative arrangements or coercive impositions by victorious powers or even efforts to move toward a new state system that would allow the development of general and complete disarmament and a demilitarization of society.

Croft also suggests that besides these forms of arms control evolving over time (type 5, for example, only appearing in the twentieth century), there have been two general processes occurring in regard to arms control as a whole. The scope of arms control has been *widening* with the growth in the range of issues to which it has been applied. More important, in recent decades arms control agreements have been subject to what he terms *deepening*—in the amount of detail incorporated, the stringency of the provisions for verification, and the degree to which mechanisms for an ongoing development of a regime are written in. In short, arms control agreements have come to cover an increasing number of problem areas and have become much more detailed and serious in their requirements of state parties. The consequences of this deepening process can be seen clearly if the 1925 Geneva Protocol is compared with the 1993 Chemical Weapons Convention. Whereas the protocol only requires state parties to forswear use of chemical weapons, the CWC adds numerous other requirements including those to destroy weapons and facilities and to establish national measures related to verification and a national organization linked to the international Organization for the Prohibition of Chemical Weapons (OPCW) (16).

THE MECHANISMS OF ARMS CONTROL

As we have seen, arms control as defined here can include coercive arrangements imposed on defeated states, or unilateral measures undertaken by sovereign states without explicit expectation of reciprocation. However, an *arms control agreement* is made between state parties in a partly cooperative and partly competitive relationship through a process of negotiation. Such agreements may be *bilateral,* as between the two superpowers in regard to their nuclear weapons during the Cold War; *global,* like the Chemical Weapons Convention between many states; or *regional,* as between the states of one of the Nuclear Weapons–Free Zones. As Goldblat points out, agreements also take many forms:

> from treaties, conventions, protocols or documents, to guidelines, memoranda, declarations or common understandings, to statutes, charters and binding decisions of international bodies or final acts of international conferences, to joint or simultaneous statements by governments, exchanges of letters or notes amongst the states concerned. (12)

Also, confusingly, as arms control agreements are part of international law, it is possible for a state that has not signed up to an agreement to nevertheless be considered as having obligations under that arms control agreement because it has become accepted as customary international law (17). Thus, the Geneva Protocol of 1925 could reasonably be said to apply universally because it has been so widely accepted by states for three quarters of a century.

The outcome of an arms control negotiation is a written text that is signed by the state parties involved in reaching the agreement. The agreement will then usually be subject to ratification by the national legislative processes of the state parties and will come into force when an agreed set of requirements (for example, a fixed number of ratifications) has been achieved. It will also be possible for states to accede to agreements at a later stage. Frequently, agreements will include arrangements for regular *review conferences,* and though state parties usually live up to the agreements they sign (not to do so would be to risk losing credibility in other dealings), there will often be a provision by which the agreement can be abrogated in the extreme circumstances of a threat to national security. Most major treaties or conventions will include a *preamble* that, while not legally binding, sets out the rationale for the agreement. The *articles* of the agreement will include both the *substantive clauses* related to the substance of the agreement and the *administrative clauses* setting out how the agreement will be operated. Although in the past it was usual to appoint a *depositary state* or *states* to take care of the agreement, the growing complexity of the requirements means it is now becoming increasingly the norm to set up an *international organization* to oversee the operation of the agreement (18). The increasing workload is particularly noticeable in relation to the huge advances made in *verification* of arms control agreements.

The content of arms control agreements will necessarily appear to be technical and military, and the process of negotiation and agreement formulation will be an issue of international law, but arms control and disarmament are above all subjects of national and international politics (19). As was amply demonstrated in the recent successful campaign to achieve an agreement on the prohibition of antipersonnel landmines, significant roles may be played by individuals, nongovernmental organizations (20), and international peace movements (21), whose achievements are sometimes marked by the award of Nobel Peace Prizes (22). It would be difficult, for example, to understand the history of arms control and disarmament in the twentieth century without some knowledge of the work of Philip Noel-Baker, whose efforts spanned the years from the League of Nations system immediately after World War I to the First United Nations Special Session on Disarmament in 1978 (23). Noel-Baker's most famous book, *The Arms Race: A Programme for World Disarmament* (1958), summarized his views and experience. Similarly, it would be difficult to understand the history of efforts to achieve nuclear disarmament since World War II without knowledge of the Pugwash movement of scientists, and its recent president, Professor Joseph Rotblat. The 1995 Nobel Peace Prize was justly awarded jointly to Professor Rotblat and the Pugwash movement for their efforts since the Russell-Einstein Manifesto of 1955 (24).

THE AGENDA OF ARMS CONTROL TODAY

We cannot know how arms control and disarmament processes will evolve to meet the challenges of the twenty-first century, but there are two characteristics of the present, transitory, post–Cold War period in the international system that will demand great attention (4, 11). First, the process of decolonization of the Western European empires and the breakup of the

Soviet Union has tripled the number of states in the international system over the past fifty years, and many of these new states are experiencing great difficulty (9). As the handbook *Peace, Security and Conflict Prevention* stresses, "[t]oday, the most likely menace is civil wars and regional conflicts. Indeed, major armed conflicts have one common denominator; they are internal in nature" (25). For this reason it is not surprising that we have seen increasing efforts to make new far-reaching agreements to prohibit antipersonnel landmines, and an increasing overlap between arms control and international peacekeeping issues (26). Given the prevalence of internal civil wars, there is obviously also a renewed emphasis on the Humanitarian Law of War—the control of conduct in warfare—embodied in the Geneva Conventions. This is manifest in current efforts by the international community to find more effective means of bringing war criminals to justice in international criminal courts. In February 1993, for example, the United Nations Security Council, in Resolution 808, established an international tribunal to prosecute persons responsible for serious violations of international humanitarian law in the former Yugoslavia (25).

The second characteristic of the current international system of particular importance here is the application of science and technology to the industrialization of warfare, a process generally acknowledged to have begun 150 years ago in the U.S. Civil War, and which continues apace (27). We are naturally most familiar with the consequences of the nuclear revolution, but it is abundantly clear that the revolution in information technology is having a major impact on military operations as well as in civil society (28). It is also clear that the revolution in modern biotechnology is generating major changes in the thinking of military organizations about the potential threat from biological weapons (29). The perception that the industrialization of warfare had increased and would further increase its destructiveness and lethality was in good part responsible for the efforts in the nineteenth century, for example, in the foundation of the International Committee of the Red Cross (ICRC) and The Hague Peace Conferences, to introduce new regulations on armaments and warfare. It is predominantly with this process of evolution of global norms (30) and international law (31) over the past 150 years that we shall be concerned here.

Following the slaughter of World War I, great efforts were made within the League of Nations system to find new agreements on arms control (32). Though the 1925 Geneva Protocol, which prohibits the use of chemical and biological weapons, remains a cornerstone in the regulation of these weapons of mass destruction, overall the League of Nations system failed. Then with World War II came the development of the strategic bombing of cities and eventually the use of atomic bombs on Hiroshima and Nagasaki. It is hardly surprising that it was difficult for the international system to find means of dealing with such developments; in ten years or so the explosive power of weapons leaped from tens of tons to kilotons (x 1,000)

and then to megatons (x 1,000,000). Initially, attempts were made to find
means of general and complete disarmament (33), but following the near
disaster of the Cuban Missile Crisis in 1962 (34), the restricted Cold War
conception of arms control set in and produced, in particular, the series of
bilateral nuclear agreements between the United States and the Soviet
Union referred to previously.

In truth, however, a massive buildup of all forms of armaments continued throughout the Cold War period (35, 36), and dealing with the consequences of that buildup—for example, safeguarding Russian nuclear
material as strategic and other nuclear weapons stockpiles are reduced—
forms a major component of the present arms control agenda (37). A second major component of the agenda must be to find effective global
treaties to restrain the *proliferation of weapons of mass destruction.*
Though the Chemical Weapons Convention has most of the attributes required, the Biological and Toxin Weapons Convention lacks any effective
mechanism for verification and an equivalent nuclear weapons convention
seems far in the future in view of the apparent determination of the nuclear
weapons states to retain their weapons (38). Yet human survival in the
longer term does not seem compatible with the widespread retention of
such destructive weaponry (39).

Thus, in broad terms the current arms control agenda is to find means
of dealing with the internal and regional warfare that has become more
prevalent since the lifting of the political stagnation imposed by the superpowers during the Cold War; to continue to seek means of dealing with the
consequences of the massive amounts of weaponry built up during the
Cold War; and to come to terms more generally with the development of
weapons of mass destruction. In this new period of multilateralism, greater
reliance will have to be placed on the role of the United Nations (12, 25)
and its related bodies such as the Conference on Disarmament in Geneva
(40). A crucial issue is whether the United Nations can meet this challenge
or whether the fate of the League of Nations awaits it. It should be understood that this is an ongoing issue and debate, as was made obvious by the
Indian and Pakistani nuclear weapons tests of 1998. It is to be expected
that arms control will continue to be the subject of major reports and studies (41), and it is to be hoped that eventually it will be possible to hold a
fourth United Nations special session on disarmament at which a framework for long-term progress can be agreed (42).

NEW BIOLOGICAL WEAPONS

It is apparent from the preceding overview that international arms control is
presently an ad hoc system that has developed in response to the perceived

problems of our particular age. Moreover, in today's world, reaching a widely accepted, multilateral agreement on a substantive topic of widespread concern is hardly likely to be achieved rapidly. Against this background, therefore, the problem of new biological weapons—the threat they pose, their proliferation and possible control—can be viewed in a clearer light.

In the twentieth century we saw a series of offensive BW programs undertaken by major states. It is beyond doubt that the "classical" biological agents weaponized in the massive U.S. program of the 1950s and 1960s are effective. These agents—such as anthrax and botulinum toxins (BTX)—remain the primary concern today because they would not require large-scale testing by a proliferator. This is quite evident from the agents chosen to be weaponized in Iraq's offensive BW program (43). From what has entered the public record, we know that the former Soviet Union's huge offensive BW program used the new genetic engineering techniques to make specific modifications to the antibiotic resistance characteristics of plague (44). This has obviously generated concern that such techniques, as they spread around the world for legitimate civil purposes, might be misused to make other specific modifications to agents. It might be possible, for example, to improve the environmental resistance of agents or to modify a benign microorganism so that it produced a damaging toxin (45). Such specific modifications, especially if used in combination, could make these dangerous agents even more usable on the battlefield or for terrorist purposes.

We can thus see that the historical process of misusing *current* biological and medical capabilities in offensive biological warfare programs continues: The genetic engineering techniques discovered in the early 1970s were misused in the former Soviet Union during the 1980s. But we are only in the initial stages of the revolution in biotechnology. The Human Genome Project—designed to uncover the full details of our genetic make-up by the early years of the twenty-first century—signifies how much further this scientific revolution and its applications have to run. There are undoubtedly dangers that the new knowledge might be misused, for example, to develop new biological weapons that could be targeted at specific genetic characteristics of different ethnic groups (46).

Chemical and biological weapons are best considered together as forming a spectrum of threat (Table 1.1) (47). Between classical man-made chemical agents such as nerve gas at one end of the spectrum, and classical, naturally occurring living biological agents such as anthrax bacteria at the other, there is some overlap in the group of naturally occurring chemicals produced by biological organisms. These so-called midspectrum agents—bioregulators and toxins—are the subjects of this book; they are appropriately intended to be covered by both the Biological and Toxin Weapons Convention and the Chemical Weapons Convention.

Table 1.1   The Chemical and Biological Warfare Threat Spectrum

Chemicals
  Classical CW: mustard gas, nerve gas
  Emerging CW: toxic industrial chemicals, toxic pharmaceutical chemicals, toxic
    agricultural chemicals
Chemicals of biological origin
  Bioregulators: peptides
  Toxins: saxitoxin, mycotoxin, ricin
Biological organisms
  Genetically manipulated BW: modified/tailored bacteria, viruses
  Traditional BW: bacteria, viruses, rickettsia

Source: Modified from reference 47.

Toxins and bioregulators have been chosen for scrutiny in part because they have a history of misuse. A stronger reason, though not widely recognized, is that the biotechnology revolution will engender a profound change in our understanding of how the human nervous system and associated endocrine and immune systems work, in which chemical messengers are increasingly understood to play very important roles (48). Misuse of this new neuroscience could provide novel means of manipulating human behavior by chemical means. In examining potential misuse of combinations of advances from different scientific fields, possible ethnic targeting of toxins and bioregulators will be considered as an extreme case.

OUTLINE OF THE BOOK

The history of the operational use of toxins and bioregulators in past offensive biological weapons programs is presented in Chapter 2. Chapter 3 reviews increasing official concerns, expressed at review conferences of the BTWC, about the potential impact of the biotechnology revolution on these kinds of weapons. Chapters 4 and 5 examine the nature and role of toxins and bioregulators in more detail. In Chapter 6 an attempt is made to link the reality of increasing specificity of toxin and bioregulatory agents—brought about through the enormous efforts devoted to understanding cell receptor systems for legitimate medical purposes—with efforts by the International Committee of the Red Cross to outlaw weapons based on such specificity.

Chapter 7 deals with the growing capabilities for agent delivery and Chapter 8 with targets. Chapter 9 then asks whether current efforts to strengthen the Biological and Toxin Weapons Convention and to implement the Chemical Weapons Convention are adequate to the task of eliminating the threat these weapons pose. Finally, Chapter 10 addresses the deeper question of how well biotechnology—which can be used equally for profoundly beneficial or profoundly malign ends—might be controlled in the coming decades.

REFERENCES

1. E. Marshall (1999). Defending against bugs and bytes. *Science* 283 (29 January): 611–612.

2. M. R. Dando (1999). The impact of the development of modern biology and medicine on the evolution of offensive biological warfare programs in the twentieth century. *Defense Analysis* 15, no. 1: 43–62.

3. D. Franz (1997). Clinical recognition and management of patients exposed to biological warfare agents. *Journal of the American Medical Association* 278, no. 5: 399–411.

4. N. Boyce (1999). A terrifying power. *New Scientist* (30 January): 10–11.

5. N. W. Gallagher (1998). Bridging the gaps on arms control. In N. W. Gallagher, ed., *Arms Control: New Approaches to Theory and Policy.* London: Frank Cass, pp. 1–24.

6. L. Freedman (1992). The end of formal arms control. In E. Adler, ed., *The International Practice of Arms Control.* Baltimore, Md.: Johns Hopkins University Press, pp. 69–84.

7. C. Smith (1998). *Nuclear Tests in South Asia.* Briefing Paper No. 69. International Security Information Service, London, June.

8. I. Daalder (1992). The future of arms control. *Survival* (spring): 51–73.

9. P. Rogers and M. R. Dando (1992). *A Violent Peace: Global Security After the Cold War.* London: Brassey's.

10. J. E. Sims (1992). The American approach to arms control. In E. Adler, ed., *The International Practice of Arms Control.* Baltimore, Md.: Johns Hopkins University Press, pp. 265–287.

11. G. J. Rattray (1996). Introduction. In J. A. Larsen and G. J. Rattray, eds., *Arms Control: Toward the 21st Century.* Boulder, Colo.: Lynne Rienner, pp. 1–18.

12. J. Goldblat (1996). *Arms Control: A Guide to Negotiations and Agreements.* London: Sage.

13. R. L. O'Connell (1995). *Ride of the Second Horseman: The Birth and Death of War.* Oxford: Oxford University Press.

14. G. Cashman (1993). *What Causes War? An Introduction to Theories of International Conflict.* New York: Lexington Books.

15. S. Croft (1996). *Strategies of Arms Control: A History and Typology.* Manchester: Manchester University Press.

16. E. A. Tanzman (1995). "Arms control and the rule of law." Paper presented to the 36th Convention of the International Studies Association, Chicago, February.

17. P. R. Trimble (1993). Legal dimensions of arms control and disarmament. In R. D. Burns, ed., *Encyclopedia of Arms Control and Disarmament.* Vol. 1. New York: Charles Scribner's Sons, pp. 371–378.

18. R. O. Keohane (1998). International institutions: Can interdependence work? *Foreign Policy* (spring): 82–96.

19. J. A. Schear (1993). Political aspects of arms control and disarmament. In R. D. Burns, ed., *Encyclopedia of Arms Control and Disarmament.* Vol. 1. New York: Charles Scribner's Sons, pp. 425–442.

20. M. E. Lord (1993). Non-governmental organisations in arms control and disarmament. In R. D. Burns, ed., *Encyclopedia of Arms Control and Disarmament*. Vol. 1. New York: Charles Scribner's Sons, pp. 405–424.

21. S. E. Cooper and L. S. Wittner (1993). Transnational peace movements and arms control: The nineteenth and twentieth centuries. In R. D. Burns, ed., *Encyclopedia of Arms Control and Disarmament*. Vol. 1. New York: Charles Scribner's Sons, pp. 491–506.

22. E. Laszlo and J. Y. You (1986). *Treaties, Chronology of the Peace Movement, Nobel Peace Prize Laureates*. Vol. 3 of *World Encyclopedia of Peace*. Oxford: Pergamon Press.

23. P. Noel-Baker (1979). *The First World Disarmament Conference 1932– 1933: And Why It Failed*. Oxford: Pergamon Press.

24. J. K. Miettinen and K. T. Takamaa (1997). *Allegiance to Humanity: Joseph Rotblat and Pugwash After 40 Years*. The Finnish Pugwash Committee, Helsinki.

25. A. D. Rotfeld et al. (1998). *Peace, Security, and Conflict Prevention: SIPRI-UNESCO Handbook*. Oxford: Oxford University Press.

26. M. R. Dando (1998). An arms control regime for the 21st century. In T. Woodhouse, R. Bruce, and M. R. Dando, eds., *Peacekeeping and Peacemaking: Towards Effective Interventions in Post–Cold War Conflicts*. London: Macmillan, pp. 103–130.

27. E. Hagerman (1988). *The American Civil War and the Origins of Modern Warfare*. Bloomington: Indiana University Press.

28. G. Stix (1995). Fighting future wars. *Scientific American* (December): 74–80.

29. M. R. Dando (1994). *Biological Warfare in the 21st Century: Biotechnology and the Proliferation of Biological Weapons*. London: Brassey's.

30. E. A. Nadelmann (1990). Global prohibition regimes: The evolution of norms in international society. *International Organization* 44, no. 4: 479–526.

31. S. R. Ratner (1998). International law: The trials of global norms. *Foreign Policy* (spring): 65–80.

32. J. Barras (1993). The League of Nations and disarmament. In R. D. Burns, ed., *Encyclopedia of Arms Control and Disarmament*. Vol. 1. New York: Charles Scribner's Sons, pp. 605–620.

33. L. D. Weiler (1986). General disarmament proposals. *Arms Control Today* (July/August): 6–15.

34. B. Allyn et al. (1990). Essence of revision: Moscow, Havana, and the Cuban Missile Crisis. *International Security* 14, no. 3: 136–172.

35. P. Rogers, M. R. Dando, and P. van den Dungen (1981). *As Lambs to the Slaughter: The Facts About Nuclear War*. London: Arrow Books.

36. M. R. Dando and P. Rogers (1984). *The Death of Deterrence*. London: CND.

37. B. Roberts (1992). Arms control and the end of the Cold War. *Washington Quarterly* (autumn): 39–56.

38. M. R. Dando (1995). Chemical and biological warfare review: Problems and prospects in building an integrated arms control regime. *Brassey's Defence Yearbook*. London: Brassey's, pp. 219–233.

39. P. Doty (1997). "Survival in the long term." Paper presented at the 47th Pugwash Conference on Science and World Affairs: Remember Your Humanity. Lillehammer, Norway, 1–7 August.

40. M. Tucker (1989). *Non-Nuclear Powers and the Geneva Conference on Disarmament: A Study in Multilateral Arms Control*. Ottawa: Canadian Institute for Peace and Security.

41. Canberra Commission (1996). *Executive Summary: Report of the Canberra Commission on the Elimination of Nuclear Weapons.* Canberra, August.

42. J. P. de Cuéllar (1988). Opening address: Third special session on disarmament. *Disarmament* 11, no. 3: 1–7.

43. UN Secretary General (1995). *Report of the Secretary General on the Status of the Implementation of the Special Commission's Plan for the Ongoing Monitoring and Verification of Iraq's Compliance with the Relevant Parts of Section C of Security Council Resolution 687 (1991).* S/1995/864. New York.

44. R. Preston (1998). Annals of warfare: The bioweaponeers. *New Yorker,* March, pp. 52–65.

45. W. Cohen (1997). *Proliferation: Threat and Response.* U.S. Department of Defense. Washington, D.C. Available online at http://www.defenselink.mil/pubs/prolif97/index.html.

46. V. Nathanson, M. Darvell, and M. R. Dando (1999). *Biotechnology, Weapons, and Humanity.* London: Harwood Academic Publishers (for the British Medical Association).

47. G. S. Pearson (1990). The CBW spectrum. *ASA Newsletter* 90: 1, 7–8.

48. M. R. Dando (1996). *A New Form of Warfare: The Rise of Non-Lethal Weapons.* London: Brassey's.

2

Operational Toxin and Bioregulatory Weapons

Because of the relative openness of U.S. society, much of the detailed information available on biological weapons comes from the records of the U.S. offensive biological weapons program that ran from World War II to the late 1960s, a period of almost two and a half decades. During that time this massive research and development effort went through a number of phases. The official U.S. Army account of the mid-1970s suggests a series of six phases following the initial work during the war (Table 2.1) (1). It is obvious from the characterization of these phases that the program was directed toward the possible operational use of the biological weapons produced.

The 1925 Geneva Protocol had outlawed the use of both chemical and biological weapons, but not their research, development, or production (2). Though the United States had stated it would not use chemical weapons except in retaliation (i.e., it would hold them as a deterrent) during World War II, it was not, at the time of its offensive biological weapons program, a signatory to the protocol. The possibility of it using chemical and biological weapons in other circumstances was made quite explicit in 1956. As the U.S. official account noted: "In 1956, a revised BW/CW policy was formulated to the effect that the US would be prepared to use BW or CW in a general war to enhance military effectiveness" (1, vol. 1). A number of biological and toxin agents were weaponized for use against humans and staple food crop plants. Our first consideration here will be the toxin weapons developed.

TOXIN WEAPONS

An official 1992 French paper prepared to consider whether the Biological and Toxin Weapons Convention could, in fact, be verified, set out the range of agents covered by the convention as follows:

17

Table 2.1   The Phases of the U.S. Offensive Biological Warfare Program

Phase	Activity
World War II	"The production plant, Vigo Ordnance Works, constructed at Terre Haute, Indiana to provide a retaliatory capability using aerial bombs, ceased operation before infectious BW agents production began" [the war had ended].
1946–1949	"From the end of World War II until 1950, no production was carried out for the purpose of operational readiness and no facilities were available for such work."
1950–1953	"The first limited BW capability was achieved in 1951 when an anticrop bomb was developed, tested and placed in production for the Air Force."
1954–1958	"[Pine Bluff Arsenal] became operational in the spring of 1954 with the first production of *Brucella suis* (the causative agent of undulant fever). Large scale production of the lethal agent *Pasteurella tularensis* [later called *Francisella tularensis*] (tularemia) began a year later."
1959–1962	"The advent of limited war and small scale conflict evoked a need for weapons which could assist in controlling conflict with minimum casualties. Controlled temporary incapacitation, therefore, became an . . . objective, and CW and BW . . . offered the most promising technical possibilities. The BW program was then shifted to emphasize incapacitation." "An anticrop weapons system for the Air Force resumed in 1962 with the production of agent. . . . The development of vaccines for Q fever and tularemia enabled development work on Q fever and tularemia to proceed to standardization as BW agents."
1963–1968	"In 1964 RDTE (Research, Development, Test, Evaluation) on enterotoxins from bacteria of the *Staphylococcus* group, which caused severe short term incapacitation . . . had progressed to the point where development of weapon systems appeared feasible. As a result, work on this potential agent was accelerated."

Source: From reference 1.

- "Living agents capable of self-reproduction: *bacteria, fungi,* etc.;
- Living agents capable of reproduction only in a host cell: *viruses;*
- *Non-living agents* incapable of reproduction, but secreted by living organisms: *peptides, toxins;*
- *Non-living agents* incapable of reproduction that are *obtained by chemical synthesis,* but whose structure is identical or very similar to that of agents in the category just mentioned" (emphases added) (3).

So a bacterium like anthrax is able to infect a host organism and reproduce itself inside that host. A virus such as smallpox, however, not only has to infect a host organism but also has to enter the cells of that organism in order to subvert the cell's machinery to reproduce itself. Nonliving agents such as toxins cannot reproduce; they are nonliving chemicals either secreted by living organisms or synthesized by scientists.

A proliferator seeking biological weapons therefore has a wide range of possible agents to choose from. The ideal agent would possess certain characteristics such as ease of production and storage, robustness on dispersal, and a known predictable effect on the intended victims (4). One possible disadvantage of biological agents such as bacteria and viruses is that, after initial infection, there is a certain time lag before they multiply and cause illness. For some purposes, a much more rapid effect might be required, and here a toxin might be used because it could be expected to act more rapidly. This would be particularly true if the toxin was used in the most effective way, that is, spread in large quantities on the wind and inhaled directly into the lungs of the intended victims. Not surprisingly, therefore, the "classical" biological agents weaponized by the United States included two toxin weapons: botulinum toxin and staphylococcal enterotoxin B (SEB). Botulinum toxin is among the most deadly substances known to humans, whereas staphylococcal enterotoxin B would act to incapacitate most victims for days, so these toxins again illustrate something of the range of possibilities open to the weapons designer.

Right from the start of the U.S. program, toxins were high on the list of potential antipersonnel agents. The official history reports: "Production of all BW agents including antipersonnel and anticrop material, was based on technology developed in laboratory and pilot plant facilities at Fort Detrick. The first pilot plant, intended for the production of botulinum toxin, was completed in October 1943" (1, vol. 2). In fact, the only facility operated for large-scale production of antipersonnel biological agents was at Pine Bluff Arsenal. Construction was completed in 1953, and then,

> [b]etween 1954 and 1967, the facility produced the following biological agents and toxins: *Brucella suis, Pasteurella tularensis,* Q fever rickettsia, Venezuelan Equine Encephalomyelitis, *Bacillus anthracis,* botulinum toxin and staphylococcal enterotoxin. . . . Bulk agents and antipersonnel munitions filled with these agents and toxins were produced and stored. (1, vol. 2)

The stocks were only finally destroyed when the U.S. offensive program was terminated at the end of the 1960s.

The general characteristics of botulinum toxin were described by Colonel William Creasy (chief, Research and Engineering Division, Office of the Chief Officer, U.S. Chemical Corps) in a presentation to an ad hoc committee of the secretary of defense in early 1950:

> When enough toxin is inhaled or ingested to produce clinical symptoms, there is a high fatality rate, death generally being rapid and medical treatment ineffective. . . . Specific anti-toxin is effective if administered before symptoms appear. An effective toxoid is available for immunization prior to exposure. The agent is not transmitted man to man. (5)

In short, this is a lethal agent that is not contagious and is fast acting in high doses. Dorothy L. Miller noted in her history of the U.S. Air Force participation in the offensive program that in 1950 botulinum toxin was among the most significant agents from a military standpoint and that considerable emphasis was being placed on it to bring it to a point where standardization in a weapons system was possible (6).

Botulism is well known outside military circles as an occasional severe form of food poisoning. The specific organism responsible for producing the deadly toxin was discovered just before the end of the nineteenth century (7). Botulism is caused by the bacterium *Clostridium botulinum,* whose spores are present in the environment. It can result from inadequate heating of food during the canning process. The spores of the bacterium are therefore not killed and can germinate and flourish in the anaerobic conditions. Botulism occurs if the contaminated food is eaten without being heated enough to destroy the toxin (8). As will be seen later, the toxin interferes with the operation of the nervous system such that the muscles of the body are unable to function properly.

Two U.S. military publications of the early 1970s detailed the way in which the toxin was to be used as a weapon. The U.S. Army's *Field Manual: Military Chemistry and Chemical Compounds* describes botulinum toxin as "the protein-like exotoxin formed by the botulinum bacillus. Through repeated purification procedures, it has been obtained in a crystalline form. . . . There are at least six distinct types: A, B, C, D, E and F. Types A, B, E and F are known to be toxic to man; types C and D are toxic to animals but very rarely to man" (9).

The summary volume on biological agents weaponized by the United States, *Toxic Agents, Part 1: Botulinum Toxin,* states that "XR" was the "[f]ormer designation of botulinum toxin, Type A. A biological agent" (10). Much of the data in this declassified volume is appropriately blacked out, but the general description of the agent and the way it was produced and intended to be used can be seen. According to this source: "XR is the agent symbol for the partially purified, spray-dried preparation of the type A botulinum toxin. The toxin is produced during growth of *C. botulinum* in a suitable medium. . . . The active protein is concentrated from the medium by isoelectric precipitation" (10).

The agent produced in this way was very impure, but as the dose of 50 percent agent required to kill 50 percent of exposed human beings (LD_{50}) was estimated to be only about 4.8 micrograms (10^{-6} grams), this did not prevent the toxin from being suitable as an agent. Moreover, it is possible to produce an antitoxin against each toxin type in order to protect friendly troops. If the dried agent is spread on the wind, there is little loss of toxicity unless there is bright sunlight, when the decay rate of the toxin is about 7.8 percent per minute. The response of an affected victim is described as very severe. The military significance of this agent needs to be understood. As the U.S. Army *Textbook of Military Medicine* points out, work on botulinum toxin was begun during World War II because it was feared that Germany might use it against invasion forces. However, a toxoid could be prepared to vaccinate people prior to exposure. Although troops were *not* actually vaccinated before D-day, large quantities of the toxoid were prepared and shipped to England for possible use (11). Fortunately, Agent XR was never used as a lethal biological agent by the United States.

One lethal toxin that certainly has been used, for assassination purposes, is ricin. Ricin is produced from beans of the castor oil plant, *Ricinis communis*, a plant that has been known to be highly toxic to humans since ancient times, and many instances of its harmful effects have been reported in the medical literature. The way in which ricin interrupts protein synthesis in the body's cells is known in some detail (12). Though ricin is about a thousand times less toxic than botulinum toxin, it is quite stable and widely available as a simple by-product of castor oil production. It might therefore be considered as a potential biological weapons agent by a proliferator. Indeed, toward the end of World War I, the United States began to study ricin as a possible agent and developed it to the stage of testing a bomb (the W bomb), in cooperation with the British, at the time of World War II. If used as a biological weapon, through inhalation of the material from an aerosol cloud, the toxin would kill by causing massive damage to the airways of its victims. One well-known example of the use of ricin for assassination was the killing of the Bulgarian dissident Georgi Markov in London in 1978 (13). While walking in London, Markov was jabbed in the thigh by the tip of an umbrella. Unknown to the doctors treating him, a small metal pellet containing ricin was left in his muscle. Markov died a few days later from the effects of the poison.

In view of our interest in the potential use of new agents to interfere with the immune system, it should be noted that Paul Ehrlich did some of the very early studies of the mammalian immune system during the 1890s by using ricin and the related toxin abrin. These related lectins are much less toxic to mice if administered orally rather than injected, so Ehrlich was able to feed animals small amounts of the toxins and show that the animals developed specific antibody proteins in the serum in response. These antibody proteins were then capable of neutralizing the toxins.

It should also be noted that such toxins are being used in medicine today. Hybrid antibody-toxin (chimeric) molecules are being developed to target cancer cells, specifically with toxin. Cancer cells have specific antibody-receptor sites on their surfaces. The idea is that specific monoclonal antibodies can be made to target these sites; if a toxin is attached to the antibody, it will be delivered directly to the cancerous cell. Clearly, such desirable developments could facilitate misuse of the same technology.

The reality of the misuse of toxins in offensive biological weapons programs was startlingly confirmed by the discovery of the Iraqi program following the 1991 Gulf War. As the detailed 1995 United Nations Special Commission (UNSCOM) report stated:

> Iraq's biological weapons programme as described to the Commission embraced a comprehensive range of agents and munitions. Agents under Iraq's biological weapons programme included lethal agents, eg anthrax, botulinum toxin and ricin, and incapacitating agents, eg aflatoxin, mycotoxins, haemorrhagic conjunctivitis virus and rotavirus. The scope of biological warfare agents worked on by Iraq encompassed both anti-personnel and anti-plant weapons. (14)

Furthermore, these agents were weaponized: "The programme covered a whole variety of biological weapons delivery means, from tactical weapons (eg 122 mm rocket and artillery shells), to strategic weapons (eg aerial bombs and Al Hussein warheads filled with anthrax, botulinum toxin and aflatoxin) and 'economic' weapons, eg wheat cover smut" (14). The exact details of this extensive program were still obscure in early 1999, the latest report available, stating, for example:

> *Clostridium botulinum* toxin, Agent A: It was not possible to verify the amount of agent A produced, placed into munitions or otherwise consumed. . . . Aflatoxin, Agent C. . . . It is not possible to verify the amount of agent C placed into munitions or warheads or otherwise consumed. . . . The question remains open regarding the aim and reasons of the choice of aflatoxin as an agent for BW. It is not clear what Iraq expected to gain as a result of its use. (15)

A later UNSCOM report goes on to state that one Iraqi military document referred to "requirements to produce liver cancer using aflatoxin and the efficacy against military and civilian targets" (15). Though aflatoxin *will* cause liver cancer, that process takes many years. Given Iraq's previous use of lethal chemicals against its Kurdish population in Halabja, an envisaged use of aflatoxin as a long-term ethnic weapon cannot be ruled out.

The weaponization of *lethal* toxins in offensive biological weapons programs remains an important issue of concern today and for the future. However, as previously noted, the United States also weaponized a *nonlethal* (incapacitating) toxin. The U.S. Army's 1975 *Field Manual: Military Chemistry and Chemical Compounds* described staphylococcal food poisoning as being produced "following the ingestion of food in which various strains of staphylococci are growing. It is usually characterized by sudden, sometimes violent, onset of severe nausea; vomiting; stomach cramps; severe diarrhea; and prostration" (9). The manual also notes that after ingestion of contaminated food, there may be a latent period of two to four hours before the symptoms appear. Those affected would clearly be severely incapacitated, but most are back to a relatively normal state after twenty-four hours and fatalities are rare. The bacterium *Staphylococcus aureus* produces a number of toxins, one of which is staphylococcal enterotoxin B. This is, in fact, an exotoxin excreted by the bacterium, but because of its effect on the human gastrointestinal tract, or enteron, it is called an enterotoxin. If SEB were to be used to best advantage as a weapon, however, it would be spread in the air so that victims *inhaled* the toxin.

An article written by U.S. Army personnel in 1997 noted: "Because of its extreme toxicity as an incapacitant, inhalation exposure to this toxin could render a high percentage of exposed personnel clinically ill, requiring medical care beginning a few hours after exposure" (16). SEB is very stable in aerosols, and because such a small amount is required to incapacitate, it could be effective many miles downwind from the site of release. The summary volume on biological agents weaponized by the United States identified the SEB toxin as "Agent PG." In batch production, it states, the agent could be obtained 70 percent pure and that there was no loss of toxicity of dry PG if it was stored at −4 °C for a year or non-refrigerated below 28 °C for two months. Ease of production and of storage were clearly important subsidiary factors in its choice as an agent. Spray-drying yielded 42 to 60 percent of particles of less than 5 microns in diameter, and these could be effectively disseminated by weapon systems. The summary volume records dissemination efficiency as:

(1) *A/B 45Y-4 Dry Agent Disseminator:* 63 percent if all aerosolized particle sizes are considered; 26 percent if less than 5 micron particles are considered.

(2) *Flettner Bomblet (Dry Agent):* 15 percent if less than 5 micron particles only are considered in this figure. A 40 percent efficiency could probably be attained in bomblets of this type if all particle sizes are considered. (17)

Such bomblets would presumably have been used in multiple numbers in a cluster bomb. SEB itself is described as a "white fluffy powder" that presumably would spread easily on the air.

The 1997 U.S. *Textbook of Military Medicine* reports that during the U.S. offensive biological warfare program, "[t]his toxin was especially attractive as a biological agent because much lower quantities were needed to produce the desired effect than were required with synthetic chemicals. The dose that is incapacitating for 50% of the human population exposed . . . was found to be 0.0004 µg/kg" (18). This amount was much, much smaller than the dose required to kill people. SEB is one of seven such enterotoxins produced by the bacterium. These substances are referred to as *superantigens* because they exert their effects through a profound overreaction by the body's immune system (19). When used as an aerosolized biological warfare agent, the incapacitation produced by SEB can be long-lasting: "The fever may last up to 5 days and range from 39.4 °C to 41.1 °C. . . . The cough may persist up to 4 weeks, and patients may not be able to return to normal functions for 2 weeks" (16).

As with many such "nonlethal" chemical agents, there is the risk that exposure of a particularly susceptible person, or receipt of a particularly heavy dose, could lead to death rather than incapacitation (20).

BIOREGULATORS

A toxin is a poison produced by a living organism, and a poison is defined as a substance that injures health or causes death when introduced into the body (21). By definition, then, a toxin is something that is not a *natural* constituent of the body that it is damaging. Living organisms, however, are complex chemical systems with multiple chemical, regulatory subsystems contained within them. A weapons designer might find it possible to attack by disrupting such natural bioregulatory systems—for example, by vastly increasing the concentration (within the living organism) of a naturally oc-curring bioregulatory chemical, or by introducing large quantities of a sub-stance that mimics its effects.

It will be recalled that biological weapons were developed in the of-fensive programs of major states for use against humans, animals, and plants. It is in attacks on plants that the use, in warfare, of bioregulatory mimics on a massive scale has been demonstrated. The major study, *The Problem of Chemical and Biological Warfare* (from the Stockholm Inter-national Peace Research Institute), reported in the 1970s:

> Chemical anti-plant agents [mimics] began to attract military interest at the time of World War II but it was not until US involvement in Viet-Nam that they came to be employed on a significant scale in combat. Here they were used either to defoliate vegetation, thus removing natural cover that might conceal the enemy, or to destroy food crops. (22)

Despite compelling evidence to the contrary, the United States maintained at the time that this action was not contrary to the 1925 Geneva Protocol and changed this position only when it moved to ratify the protocol and the BTWC in 1974 (23, 24, 25).

The U.S. Army's field manual, *Military Chemistry and Chemical Compounds,* stated: "Herbicides are chemicals that possess a high poten-tial for destroying or seriously limiting the production of food and defoli-ating vegetation. The compounds kill or inhibit the growth of plants" (9). The manual divided such synthetic herbicides into five categories:

1. Plant-growth regulators that promote, inhibit, or otherwise modify physiological processes in plants—sometimes causing plant death;
2. Defoliants that prematurely remove leaves from plants;
3. Desiccants that dry up plant foliage;
4. Soil sterilants that prevent the growth of green plants when present in the soil;
5. Surface-active agents that enhance the wetting, sticking, or spreading of antiplant compounds on plants and facilitate their dispersion (9).

We are obviously interested here in the first of these. The two main agents of this category are 2,4-dichlorophenoxyacetic acid (2,4-D) and 2,4,5-trichlorophenoxyacetic acid (2,4,5-T). Their effects on plants are severe and rapid:

> Plant responses appear within 1 hour on actively growing sensitive plants. Leaf and stem curvatures are the first discernible effects. Plant injury will usually be evident within 24 hours. 2,4-D produces injury to all broadleaf plant species such as cotton, sweet potatoes, beans, sugar beets, Irish potatoes, flax, nut and fruit trees and soybeans. (9)

The notorious herbicide Agent Orange was a 50:50 mixture of the n-butyl esters of 2,4,5-T and 2,4-D. It was absorbed by plant leaves and moved internally in the plant system to the aerial growing points and the roots. In contrast to these artificial *bioregulatory* mimics, Agent Blue (an organic arsenic compound) killed by simple physical absorption of moisture from the leaves of the plant when it was sprayed onto them. The foliage dried up and shriveled.

One of the major accounts of the U.S. involvement in Vietnam was *Vietnam: A History,* written by Stanley Karnow. In the first chapter, "The War Nobody Won," Karnow graphically illustrated the dimensions of the tragedy for both sides. Recalling a report he had written of the first killing of U.S. military advisers in 1959, six years before U.S. involvement became serious, he pointed out that no one at that time could have predicted that 58,000 Americans would lose their lives (26). He continued: "Nor did I then . . . even remotely envision the holocaust that would devastate Vietnam during the subsequent sixteen years of war. More than 4 million Vietnamese soldiers and civilians on both sides—roughly 10 percent of the entire population—were to be killed or wounded" (26).

This then is the background to the large-scale use of herbicides in Vietnam, one of major modern warfare spread over many years, from the arrival of the first U.S. combat troops in Vietnam in 1965 to their departure in early 1973, and the final U.S. exit from Saigon before its capture by the northern forces in April 1975. The whole era can best be seen as falling into distinct periods. The first was the decade when U.S. personnel were only acting as advisers and ended with the arrival of U.S. combat troops in 1965. The next was the period—up to the Tet offensive in 1968—during which the United States sought ways to win the war (27). The final period involved the prolonged search for a way out, which culminated with the massive bombing of North Vietnam at Christmas 1972. Then the South Vietnamese were left to fight out the final years of the war alone.

The United States had, in fact, placed itself into an impossible strategic position. This was precisely foretold in late 1961 by General Maxwell Taylor, in a warning to President Kennedy: "If the first contingent is not enough to accomplish the necessary results, it will be difficult to resist the pressure to reinforce. If the ultimate result sought is the closing of the frontiers and the clear up of the insurgents . . . there is no limit to our possible commitments (unless we attack the source in Hanoi)" (27).

But though the United States was willing to bomb the north, it was not willing to invade for fear of drawing in China (as had happened so dramatically in the Korean War). It thus became involved in what has been described as an escalating military stalemate. In such circumstances, there is likely to be a search for more and more drastic methods of defeating the enemy. Given the technological nature of U.S. society, and its military, some of the proposed solutions were always likely to involve the use of novel technology.

The herbicide program in Vietnam had a long history. In the 1880s Charles Darwin had observed that plants bend toward the light and had therefore speculated that the tip of the plant transmitted a substance that directed the growth of the lower part of the plant. An extract of such a substance was eventually found by plant physiologists in the 1920s, and a series of potent growth-regulating chemicals were discovered during the 1930s (28). During World War II, it was suggested by U.S. scientists that synthetic growth regulators applied in abnormal quantities could be used to limit the growth of, or destroy, crops. By the end of the war the U.S. military had tested over a thousand potential defoliants (29). Parallel work in the civil sector led to the marketing of the first commercial weedkiller in the United States just after the war. This was the Chemical Paint Company's "Weedone," which used 2,4-D, and production rapidly increased in the United States for civil purposes.

The military testing program for herbicidal chemicals continued in the United States after World War II, and about 12,000 growth regulators and desiccants were studied. Large-scale field trials of some of these chemicals were carried out in the 1950s (30). However, it was the British military who had first attempted to use herbicides for clearing vegetation (to avoid the danger of ambush along lines of communication) and for crop destruction in their war against insurgents in Malaya in the 1950s (31). U.S. use of herbicides in Vietnam began on a small scale prior to the involvement of U.S. combat troops but then led to massive use during the 1960s. This chemical assault on the environment was part of the larger impact of U.S. military operations, which also included the use of high-explosive munitions and mechanized land clearance (32). The same two types of objectives were pursued as in the British campaign in Malaya, but on a much larger scale. Most herbicides were applied to noncrop areas in order to deny cover, but attempts were made, on a lesser scale, to destroy food crops (Table 2.2).

It is important to note that the concentrations of chemicals used in Vietnam far exceeded those that would be allowed for use in the United States:

> In Vietnam, Orange has been used at an average rate of some 33 kg. per hectare. . . . In the case of Orange this means that the military application rate of 2,4-D and 2,4,5-T together has been about 50 times the usual application rate of 2,4-D or 2,4,5-T in the United States (where this combination of ingredients, moreover, is not permitted at all). (30)

With the extreme care urged on users of the domestic applications and concentrations, for example "[a]void contact with skin, eyes or clothes," "[a]void inhaling dust," and so on, the safety of the military undertaking was naturally questioned at the time by many scientists.

The effects of using bioregulators in such quantities were well understood for *individual* plants. Yet the consequences of applying such substances in military quantities to fragile ecosystems were not well understood. Though the effects of herbicide use on the Vietnamese population and U.S. personnel do not appear to have been as severe as once feared (these products were contaminated during manufacturing with small quantities of the extremely poisonous chemical dioxin), ecological effects in Vietnam persisted long after the war (33). The complex mangrove ecosystem was the worst affected; even a single attack with these herbicides left

Table 2.2   U.S. Herbicide Usage by Type of Mission

Type of Mission	Usage in Thousands of Liters[a]		
	Agent Orange	Agent White[b]	Agent Blue
Forest and other vegetation	40,525	19,623	1,996
Crop	3,813	212	6,185
Total	44,338	19,835	8,182

Source: From reference 31.
Notes: a. To convert volume data to area coverage in hectares, multiply by 35.6.
b. Another herbicide containing 2,4-D.

almost nothing alive (31). The diverse plant species of this ecosystem were highly sensitive to the herbicides, and the dominant mangrove tree genus particularly so. Moreover: "Little if any immediate recolonization occurred on the herbicide-obliterated sites. With the primary producers essentially wiped out, their energy-capturing function was lost and all else that built on this" (31). So the end result of this use of bioregulatory chemicals was, in fact, the destruction of large areas of an entire ecosystem.

Study of plant-growth regulators for civil purposes had led to the development of novel chemical herbicides in the United Kingdom, as well as in the United States during the 1940s (34). The importance of weed control in agriculture stimulated research that led to major scientific and technological developments. Understanding the impact of such developments is crucial to assessing the potential threat of biological weapons in the future. The financial rewards of using herbicides were quite clear-cut: "The use of herbicides in the developed countries has been particularly successful, with an estimated near maximum market penetration in major crops. . . . Indeed estimates suggest that each dollar spent in the USA on pesticides results in an additional income of four dollars to the farmer" (35).

With that kind of incentive, scientific research and development have intensified over the past half century. This process can only accelerate as the biotechnology revolution continues to affect our understanding of plant genomics. The process of discovering new chemicals is time-consuming, but it is very systematic and eventually productive.

The methodology for seeking new herbicides involves three approaches: "(a) the rational design of specific inhibitors of key metabolic processes, (b) the use of known herbicides or phytotoxic products as lead compounds for further synthesis, and (c) the random screening of new chemicals" (35). Three levels of screens are employed:

> The *primary screen* aims to establish lead structures, namely those with sufficient activity against target species at a suitably low dose to warrant further study. . . .
> It is the aim of the *secondary screen* to optimize these initial observations by further chemistry to yield compounds with the desired characteristics for commercial potential [i.e., route b]. . . .
> *Field screens* are used to test hypotheses formulated in laboratory and glasshouse testing, and so confirm that molecules are as active in the field as initially predicted. (35)

Though rational design of new commercial products is still rather unlikely, random screening of new chemicals to discover those that have some desired effect, and the chemical manipulation of such "lead" chemicals to improve their characteristics, does work.

To maximize the desired characteristics of an herbicide, it is necessary to understand how that works. Plant hormones, which include auxins, are "naturally occurring substances, effective in very small amounts, that act as signals to stimulate or inhibit growth or regulate some developmental program. They are all small molecules, with molecular weights under 1000" (36). An optimal level of auxin normally *promotes* growth, but the supra-optimal level of auxin applied to a plant as an herbicide in substances like 2,4-D and 2,4,5-T, *synthetic* (or exogenous) *auxins,* triggers the release of another plant hormone, ethylene, which induces the desired outcome—inhibition of the growth of certain types of plants such as weeds (35).

Not surprisingly, the opening up of a new scientific field, with potentially rewarding commercial applications, has led to a stream of discoveries. Not all botanists equate plant hormones directly with animal hormones because their effects appear to be less specific, but it is generally accepted that there are at least five types of plant hormones (Table 2.3) (37).

Another reason to expect further scientific research on plant hormones is that their action is often disrupted by plant diseases (38). The net result, of course, is that an attack on plants using synthetic chemicals could be carried out today on the basis of a much more systematic and effective knowledge base than that which underpinned the U.S. program in Vietnam. As will become apparent, concerns are increasing about possible direct attack on humans through similar disruption of their chemical regulatory systems.

Table 2.3   Plant Hormones and Their Functions

Hormone Type	Example	Function
Auxin	Indole-3-acetic acid (IAA)	Stimulates stem elongation
Cytokinins	Zeatin	Stimulates cell division and growth
Gibberellins	Gibberellic acid (GA_3)	Stimulates germination of seeds
Abcisic acid	(type/example)	Closes stomata during drought
Ethylene	(type/example)	Promotes fruit ripening

Source: From reference 37.

DELIBERATE DIRECT ATTACKS
ON HUMAN CHEMICAL REGULATORY SYSTEMS

The names of the lethal chemical weapons agents developed during the twentieth century—choking agents, blood agents, blister agents, nerve agents—strongly suggest that they were designed to disrupt particular functions or systems in the human body. The modern nerve agents, for example, directly disrupt the operation of the nervous system (20). Within an individual nerve cell, information is transmitted *electrically* along its length by means of nerve impulses, but most nerve cells transmit information to other nerve or muscle cells *chemically* by releasing chemical substances at their terminals or endings. These naturally occurring substances, called neurotransmitters, obviously have to be broken down once they have fulfilled their designated function or the nerve or muscle cell they operate upon would be continuously stimulated. Acetylcholine is one particularly important transmitter, and it is normally broken down by an enzyme called acetylcholinesterase. A nerve agent such as VX binds to, and thus inactivates, this enzyme. The resulting continuous stimulation of many nerves and muscles leads to rapid death after a minute dose of such a chemical agent.

As will be seen in later chapters, most scientists would, for the sake of clarity, wish to restrict the term *transmitter* to substances like acetylcholine, which act very close to nerve endings. They would tend to reserve the term *bioregulator* for substances like hormones, which act over somewhat greater distances from their site of origin. Such careful use of terminology is good for clear scientific analysis, but it has to be understood that even lethal foreign agents like VX have quite specific disruptive chemical actions on the nervous system. In short, there is not a great deal of difference between attacking the nervous system with a chemical nerve agent and disrupting it with an excessive amount of a bioregulatory mimic. Attempting to separate lethal chemical warfare agents from the concept of disruption of bioregulatory systems becomes even more difficult in regard to other chemical, but nonlethal, agents such as BZ (U.S. Army code name for a chemical agent that produces disorientation and hallucination when inhaled).

BZ was weaponized by the United States in the 1960s and has very complex actions on the central nervous system (CNS). In the future it may come to be viewed as an early example of a range of new means of disrupting the normal functioning of the human nervous system (20). Such disruption will be considered in more detail after outlining how international arms control has been developed in an attempt to prevent this misuse of scientific knowledge.

REFERENCES

1. U.S. Army (1977). *U.S. Army Activities in the U.S. Biological Warfare Programs.* Vols. 1 and 2. Washington, D.C.: Department of the Army.

2. M. R. Dando (1999). The development of international legal constraints on biological warfare in the 20th century. In M. Koskenniemi et al., eds., *The Finnish Yearbook of International Law.* Vol. 8. The Hague: Martinus Nijhoff, pp. 1–69.

3. France (1992). *Potentially Weaponizable Biological Agents: A Tentative Typology.* Ad Hoc Group of Government Experts to Identify and Examine Potential Verification Measures from a Scientific and Technical Standpoint. BWC/CONF.III/ VEREX/WP.13, Geneva, 1 April.

4. M. R. Dando (1994). *Biological Warfare in the 21st Century: Biotechnology and the Proliferation of Biological Weapons.* London: Brassey's.

5. W. M. Creasy (1950). *Presentation to the Secretary of Defense's Ad Hoc Committee on CEBAR.* Joint Chiefs of Staff, The Pentagon, Washington D.C., 24 February.

6. D. L. Miller (1952). *History of Air Force Participation in Biological Warfare Program 1944–1951.* Historical Study No. 194. Historical Office, Office of the Executive, Air Materiel Command, Wright Patterson Air Force Base, Dayton, Ohio, September.

7. M. J. Pelczar et al. (1993). *Microbiology: Concepts and Applications.* New York: McGraw-Hill.

8. L. M. Prescott et al. (1990). *Microbiology.* Dubuque, Iowa: Wm. C. Brown.

9. U.S. Army (1975). *Field Manual: Military Chemistry and Chemical Compounds* (FM3-9). Headquarters, Department of the Army, Washington D.C., October.

10. U.S. Army (1982). *Toxic Agents.* Vol. 6 of *Joint CB* [chemical/biological] *Technical Data Source Book, Part 1: Botulinum Toxin.* Dugway Proving Ground, Utah, June.

11. J. L. Middlebrook and D. Franz (1997). Botulinum toxins. In F. R. Sidell et al., eds., *Textbook of Military Medicine, Part I: Medical Aspects of Chemical and Biological Warfare.* Washington, D.C.: Office of the Surgeon General, Department of the Army, pp. 643–654.

12. D. Franz and N. K. Jaax (1997). Ricin toxin. In F. R. Sidell et al., eds., *Textbook of Military Medicine, Part I: Medical Aspects of Chemical and Biological Warfare.* Washington, D.C.: Office of the Surgeon General, Department of the Army, pp. 631–642.

13. B. Knight (1979). Ricin—A potent homicidal poison. *British Medical Journal* 3 (February): 35–51.

14. UN Secretary General (1995). *Report of the Secretary General on the Status of the Implementation of the Special Commission's* [UNSCOM's] *Plan for the Ongoing Monitoring and Verification of Iraq's Compliance with the Relevant Parts of Section C of Security Council Resolution 687 (1991).* S/1995/864.

15. United Nations (1999). Letter from the Executive Chairman of UNSCOM to the President of the Security Council. S/1999/94. 25 January.

16. D. Franz et al. (1997). Clinical recognition and management of patients exposed to biological warfare agents. *Journal of the American Medical Association* 278, no. 5: 399–411.

17. U.S. Army (1973). *Toxic Agents.* Vol. 6 of *Joint CB Technical Data Source Book. Part 2: Agent PG.* Deseret Test Center, Fort Douglas, Utah, February.

18. R. G. Ulrich et al. (1997). Staphylococcal enterotoxin B and related pyrogenic toxins. In F. R. Sidell et al., eds., *Textbook of Military Medicine, Part I: Medical Aspects of Chemical and Biological Warfare.* Washington, D.C.: Office of the Surgeon General, Department of the Army, pp. 621–630.

19. M. R. Dando (1999). The impact of the development of modern biology and medicine on the evolution of offensive biological warfare programs in the twentieth century. *Defense Analysis* 15, no. 1: 43–62.

20. M. R. Dando (1996). *A New Form of Warfare: The Rise of Non-Lethal Weapons.* London: Brassey's.

21. A. Isaacs, et al., eds. (1989). *The Macmillan Encyclopedia.* London: Guild Publishing.

22. J. Perry Robinson (1991). *The Rise of CB Weapons.* Vol. 1 of *The Problem of Chemical and Biological Warfare.* Stockholm: Almqvist and Wiksell (for SIPRI).

23. J. Goldblat (1970). Are tear gas and herbicides permitted weapons? *Bulletin of the Atomic Scientists* (April): 13–16.

24. F. Ikle (1974). *U.S. Policy Change on Chemical Herbicides and Riot Control Agents.* Washington, D.C.: U.S. Arms Control and Disarmament Agency, 10 December.

25. F. V. Harbour (1990). *Chemical Arms Control: The U.S. and the Geneva Protocol of 1925.* Case Studies in Ethics and International Affairs. New York: Carnegie Council on Ethics and International Affairs.

26. S. Karnow (1983). *Vietnam: A History.* London: Century Publishing.

27. D. R. Palmer (1978). *Summons of the Trumpet: A History of the Vietnam War from a Military Man's Viewpoint.* New York: Ballantine Books.

28. J. B. Neilands et al. (1972). *Harvest of Death: Chemical Warfare in Vietnam and Cambodia.* London: Collier-Macmillan.

29. P. F. Cecil (1986). *Herbicidal Warfare: The RANCH HAND Project in Vietnam.* New York: Praeger.

30. W. D. Verwey (1977). *Riot Control Agents and Herbicides in War.* Leyden, The Netherlands: A. W. Sijthoff.

31. A. H. Westing (1984). *Herbicides in War: The Long-term Ecological and Human Consequences.* London: Taylor and Francis (for SIPRI).

32. A. H. Westing (1976). *Ecological Consequences of the Second Indochina War.* Stockholm: Almqvist and Wiksell (for SIPRI).

33. W. M. A. Hay (1998). "Defoliants: The long-term health implications." Paper presented to the 1st International Conference on Addressing Environmental Consequences of War: Legal, Economic, and Scientific Prospectus. Washington, D.C., 10–12 June.

34. R. J. Stephens (1982). *Theory and Practice of Weed Control.* London: Macmillan.

35. A. Cobb (1992). *Herbicides and Plant Physiology.* London: Chapman and Hall.

36. D. E. Fosket (1994). *Plant Growth and Development: A Molecular Approach.* San Diego: Academic Press.

37. R. Moore et al. (1995). *Botany.* Dubuque, Iowa: Wm. C. Brown.

38. P. G. Ayres ed. (1981). *The Effects of Disease on the Physiology of the Growing Plant.* Cambridge: Cambridge University Press.

3

Concerns About the Misuses of Biotechnology

In early 1999 the British journal *New Scientist* carried a report from the annual meeting of the American Association for the Advancement of Science (AAAS) in Anaheim, California. Under the heading, "A Terrifying Power," it was reported that "[t]he world's first simple artificial life form could be constructed in the next few years" (1). But, the article went on to say, "the team leading the way have stopped work for the moment, fearing that their discovery might lead to the creation of the ultimate bioweapon in the shape of a synthetic 'superbug'" (1).

So just three decades after it was demonstrated that genetic engineering—the movement of functional genes between different species—was possible, it was being claimed that entirely artificial life could be created by biologists. This was no idle claim, as *New Scientist* explained, for the project to create an artificial life form was being carried out by Craig Venter and his colleagues at the Institute for Genomic Research in Rockville, Maryland; the group was responsible for describing the first complete deoxyribonucleic acid (DNA) sequence of a cellular organism, that of *Haemophilus influenzae,* in 1995. In later work, which compared the genomes (DNA sequences) of simple microorganisms, they had identified about 300 genes that appeared necessary for life. In theory at least, "they could now build an artificial chromosome carrying these genes and wrap it up in a membrane with a few proteins and other biochemicals to create a simple synthetic organism" (1).

The genomes of numerous human pathogens are also currently being worked out (2). It might therefore be possible to discover what makes them so dangerous to us and to transfer such characteristics into an artificial life form.

By way of a coincidence, also some three decades ago, the Biological and Toxin Weapons Convention was agreed in the early 1970s. Its aim was to prevent the misuse of biology in the production of just such terrifying bioweapons. Unfortunately, the convention—agreed during the middle years of the long East-West Cold War—lacked any verification provisions to ensure that the state parties were living up to their obligations. The state parties, however, have gradually come to realize how dangerous the malign implications of the revolution in biotechnology (genetic engineering) might be. Now at the beginning of the twenty-first century, they appear to be nearing the agreement of a verification protocol for the BTWC (3). It is necessary to carefully reconsider what has come to be perceived as such a threat that this amendment to the BTWC is required.

THE BIOLOGICAL AND TOXIN WEAPONS CONVENTION

The fact that biological agents and toxins could be very effective as weapons against humans, animals, and plants was quite obvious from the experts' report produced for the United Nations in the run-up to the agreement of the BTWC in the early 1970s (4). That biological weapons have to be considered as potential weapons of mass destruction is equally evident from the more technical report of the World Health Organization, produced in the same period (5). This report stated, for example, that "[i]f a biological agent such as anthrax were used, an attack on a city by even a single bomber disseminating 50 kg of the dried agent in a suitable aerosol form would affect an area far in excess of 20 km², with tens to hundreds of thousands of deaths" (4).

It was recognized that the dangers of production and use of such weapons had recently increased; the UN report concluded in part that "[t]he present inquiry has shown that the potential for developing an armoury of chemical and bacteriological (biological) weapons has grown considerably in recent years, not only in terms of the number of agents but in their toxicity and in the diversity of their effects" (4). And this was all *before* the advent of genetic engineering.

The BTWC was opened for signature in 1972 and entered into force in March 1975. Article I of the convention stated:

> Each State Party to this Convention undertakes never in any circumstances to develop, produce, stockpile or otherwise acquire or retain:
>   1. Microbial or other biological agents, or toxins whatever their origin or method of production, of types and in quantities that have no justification for prophylactic, protective or other peaceful purposes. (4)

This sweeping "General Purpose Criterion" clearly does not just relate to the *misuse* of the technology available at that time but to the *purpose* of misuse then, now, or in the future (3). Though the BTWC has lacked effective verification provisions, it has been possible for the state parties to assess the potential impact of new technological developments at the review conferences of the convention held at approximately five-year intervals. These conferences took place in 1980, 1986, 1991, and 1996 and have reflected an increasing level of concern among the state parties.

The final declaration of the First Review Conference in 1980 concluded that "[t]he Conference believes that Article I has proved sufficiently comprehensive to have covered recent scientific and technological developments relevant to the Convention" (6). This was in line with the paper on new scientific and technological developments prepared by the depositary governments—the United States, the Soviet Union, and the United Kingdom—for the review. This paper had obviously recognized the importance of the new developments:

> Even though more efficient and more specific than classical genetic techniques, recombinant DNA techniques are similar in principle. Recombinant DNA techniques do, however, permit the transfer of genetic material between widely-divergent species; classical genetic techniques generally require considerable homology between the donor and recipient for genetic transfer to be possible. (7)

The paper had also noted that specific modifications of biological agents might be possible: "[R]ecombinant DNA techniques might be used to modify the characteristics of an existing organism to increase its potential as a biological warfare agent or its ability to produce a toxin" (7). However, it concluded that "the resulting agents are unlikely to have advantages over known natural agents sufficient to provide compelling new motives for illegal production or military use" (7). The paper also predicted, in contrast to the view of present-day biologists, that "now and for the foreseeable future, development and production of fundamental new agents or toxins would present a problem of insurmountable complexity" (7).

Such conclusions would have been the result, in part, of intensive analyses within each of these states prior to the review. One such U.S. study from the early 1980s examined the feasibility of "the Warsaw Pact Nations producing new biological warfare agents by using recombinant DNA techniques to convert nonpathogenic bacteria to pathogens" (8). However, a range of difficulties was envisaged:

- Incorporating the spectrum of virulence factors required for a virulent pathogen;
- Obtaining effective expression of foreign genes;
- Maintaining the foreign genes in the host cell; and
- Avoiding a weakening of the new microorganism so it can still survive environmental stresses in the aerosolized state and resist and overcome human body defenses (8).

It was thus concluded that "the use of recombinant DNA techniques to produce new biological weapons is a complicated task that would be exceedingly difficult and probably infeasible" (8). It was also concluded that efforts to enhance the pathogenicity of known agents was likely to encounter similar difficulties. However, there did seem to be one very clear and present danger. As the study commented: "A more feasible use of recombinant DNA than the creation of new pathogens is the cheap manufacture of toxins. This is because toxins could probably be manufactured by newly created bacterial strains under controlled laboratory conditions" (8).

In short, the gene for a toxin could be engineered into an organism that in turn could be easily grown in bulk, and large amounts of toxin could thus be readily obtained. Furthermore, tremendous progress was being made in civil production technology. Another U.S. study, *Technologic Changes Since 1972: Implications for a Biological Warfare Convention*, noted in 1986: "Significant progress has taken place in the last 10 years in the productivity of fermentation plants. Much of this progress has been driven by the application of computers to process control" (9). Applications of information technology to the control of fermentation processes had allowed many more organisms to be grown successfully at high concentrations under controlled conditions.

It is not surprising that concerns over the easier production of militarily significant quantities of toxins were reflected in the final declaration of the Second Review Conference of the BTWC in 1986. The declaration first drew attention to the general problem:

> The Conference, conscious of apprehensions arising from relevant scientific and technological developments, inter alia, in the fields of microbiology, genetic engineering and biotechnology, and the possibilities of their use for purposes inconsistent with the objectives and the provisions of the Convention, reaffirms that the undertakings given by the States Parties in Article I applies to all such developments. (6)

It then dealt specifically with toxins:

> The Conference reaffirms that the Convention unequivocally applies to all natural or *artificially created microbial or other biological agents or toxins whatever their origin or method of production*. Consequently, toxins (both proteinaceous and non-proteinaceous) of a microbial, animal or vegetable nature and their synthetically produced analogues are covered. (emphasis added) (6)

There would obviously have been further detailed studies by governments of the developing biotechnology revolution and its implications in the years following the Second Review Conference (10).

The UK contribution to the background document on scientific and technological developments for the Third Review Conference of the BTWC in 1991 pointed out that not only had production of toxins become easier, but because their molecular structure was also becoming better understood, they were increasingly being used in medical applications. For example, "botulinum toxin has recently been fully licensed for treatment of various dystonias, and a technique still in the research stages is the use of ricin targeted against tumour cells by means of specific antibodies—a concept that has been called the 'magic bullet'" (11).

Similar points were made in the papers by Sweden and Australia, and the contribution by the United States concluded bluntly, "Improvements in biotechnology since the previous Review Conference [lead] us to believe that . . . potent toxins . . . can now be produced in kilogram quantities which could be militarily significant" (11).

The Canadian contribution to the background document simply noted that it had provided a separate document entitled *Novel Toxins and Bioregulators: The Emerging Scientific and Technological Issues Relating to Verification and the Biological and Toxin Weapons Convention* (12). There will be cause to consider this document in detail in a later chapter. For the moment it is necessary only to note the careful distinction it made between toxins and bioregulators:

> Toxins are highly effective and specific poisonous chemical substances isolated from living organisms. Bioregulators are naturally-occurring chemical substances, usually peptides, involved in the regulation of metabolic, physiological and possibly neural activities. Such bioregulators have also been referred to as neuropeptides or neuroregulators. (12)

More important, scientific advances were seen as proceeding rapidly in regard to both categories of chemicals: "A rapidly expanding area of research involves identifying and synthesising new bioregulators and toxins. Synthetic derivatives or slightly modified forms of these compounds can have drastically altered and toxic effects, and this could be important in the development of novel toxic agents" (12).

The contribution of the United States to the background document for the Third Review Conference also paid particular attention to peptide bioregulators:

> Peptides are precursors of proteins made up of amino acids. . . . Their range of activity covers the entire living system, from mental processes (e.g. endorphins) to many aspects of health such as control of mood, consciousness, temperature control, sleep, or emotions, exerting regulatory effects on the body. Even a small imbalance in these natural substances

could have serious consequences, inducing fear, fatigue, depression or in-capacitation. These substances would be extremely difficult to detect but could cause serious consequences or even death if used improperly. (11)

The views of the United States had to be taken very seriously because its military had long investigated the potential of chemical agents to disrupt such natural functions, and the underlying strength of its biological sciences placed it at the forefront of advances—for example, in the control of fatigue (13, 14).

The concern about possible modification of toxins and bioregulators was reflected in the changed wording of the final declaration of the Third Review Conference: "The Conference also reaffirms that the Convention unequivocally covers all microbial or other biological agents or toxins, naturally or artificially created *or altered,* whatever their origin or method of production" (emphasis added) (15).

The insertion of the words "or altered" was clearly covering the kinds of "drastically altered" effects pointed out as a possibility in modified agents by the Canadians. It is notable that the United States repeated exactly the same warning on peptide bioregulators in its contribution to the background document on scientific and technological developments for the Fourth Review Conference of the BTWC in 1996 (16).

Following the Third Review Conference, detailed studies of the military implications of the ongoing revolution in biology continued in countries with major biotechnology capabilities (17). In its contribution to the background document for the Fourth Review Conference, Switzerland, for example, argued that "[t]hese scientific and technological developments are still covered by the scope of Article I of the Convention" (16). But it continued: "However, genetically manipulated micro-organisms, unknown viruses, biological toxins, bioregulators and biochemicals still have an increased importance as potential biological warfare agents. Such weapons can be covertly produced and stored on small sites" (17). Moreover, it added: "The methods of bio- and genetechnology became widespread and are therefore more and more accessible to less experienced scientists, which enhances the danger of proliferation of BW technologies" (16). Similar concerns are clearly discernible in the contributions of other countries.

What is nevertheless striking about the background document for the Fourth Review Conference is the impact of the developing Human Genome Project and its implications for medical practice. The UK noted:

It is predicted that the human genome will be sequenced by the year 2005. The information is expected to lead to radical new treatments for a broad range of human diseases, but it may also provide information about biochemical pathways that are susceptible to peptides and other compounds, which could thus be exploited as a hostile act to damage human health. (16)

The Human Genome Project is important because it provides the basis for an objectively manipulable biological science. This will obviously have enormous benefits for medicine and agriculture, but it also opens up many more possibilities of specific malign misuse of biology for the development of new weaponry (18). All current information suggests that the HGP is reaching its goals at an accelerating rate, as scientific understanding and technology develop in tandem (Table 3.1) (19).

Table 3.1   Some Goals of the Human Genome Project for 1998–2003

Area	Goals
Genetic map	Completed
Physical map	Completed
DNA sequence	One-third finished by end 2001; working draft of the rest by end 2001; completed by 2003
Sequencing technology	Integrate and further low-cost automation
Human sequence variation[a]	100,000 mapped single nucleotide polymorphisms; develop technology
Gene identification	Full-length cDNAs [complementary DNA]
Functional analysis[a]	Develop genomic-scale technologies
Model organisms' complete DNA sequences	*Escherichia coli,* published Sept. 1997; yeast, released Apr. 1996; *Caenorhabditis elegans,* completed Dec. 1998; *Drosophila,* to be completed 2002; mouse, to be completed 2005

Source: From reference 19.
Note: a. New goals.

Little wonder then that the final declaration of the Fourth Review Conference drew specific attention to the implications of "molecular biology" and "any applications resulting from genome studies":

> The Conference, conscious of apprehensions arising from relevant scientific and technological developments, inter alia, in the fields of microbiology, biotechnology, *molecular biology,* genetic engineering, and *any applications resulting from genome studies,* and the possibilities of their use for purposes inconsistent with the objectives and the provisions of the Convention, reaffirms that the undertaking given by the States Parties in Article I applies to all such developments. (emphases added) (20)

We can expect this concern about the implications of the central thrust of modern biology and its applications to persist for many decades to come, because we are currently in the early stages of the biotechnology revolution, a revolution that must have profound—fundamental—implications for the societies in which we live (21).

It is within the general context of an integrated set of biomedical developments that particular advances and their potential implications have to be set. Thus, the UK's contribution to the background paper for the Fourth Review Conference pointed out that

> such are the advances in cloning success rates that at least the protein toxins can now, in principle, be produced on a large scale by growth of a recombinant microbial or eukaryotic cell host using well-established fermentation technology. *The genetic sequences of such toxins have been deposited in public domain molecular biology databases which are growing exponentially.* (emphasis added) (16)

The Swedish contribution also pointed to a related civil development:

> Within the pharmaceutical industry research is intense for methods to stabilize drugs for aerosol delivery of, for example, toxins, chimeric toxins, modulators of the immune system and bioregulators [all for therapeutic use]. The outcome of this research could also increase the attraction to develop more stable BTW agents. (16)

So the genetic sequences of toxins are publicly available and mass production is possible. Aerosol delivery systems are improving, and, the UK's contribution added, "[m]uch more is now known about the structure-function relationships of various toxin groups" (16). Against this background it is possible to see why the final declaration of the Fourth Review Conference was amended from that of the Third. The Fourth Review final declaration read:

> The Conference also reaffirms that the Convention unequivocally covers all microbial or other biological agents or toxins, naturally or artificially created or altered, *as well as their components,* whatever their origin or method of production, of types and in quantities that have no justification for prophylactic, protective or other peaceful purposes. (emphasis added) (16)

The addition of the words "as well as their components" allowed for the possibility that just the active part of a toxin or bioregulator or synthetic mimic might be produced for malign purposes.

It is difficult to avoid the conclusion that the records of the four Review Conferences of the BTWC actually tell a story of increasing worries about the possible misuse of *any* new relevant knowledge in offensive biological weapons programs. These concerns are reinforced by considering the way in which such new knowledge has been steadily misused over the past century, since scientists such as Louis Pasteur and Robert Koch initiated the revolution in bacteriology by demonstrating that specific microorganisms (and toxins) caused specific diseases in humans, animals, and plants (22). Such concerns appear to lie behind the U.S. Department of Defense's technical annex to its publication *Proliferation: Threat and Response,* of late 1997, which correctly argued that "[c]lassic biological warfare threat agents pose the greatest concern for the near and mid-term" (23). It is obvious, for example, from Iraq's offensive biological weapons program, that there would be considerable advantages for a proliferator in going first for agents such as anthrax and botulinum toxin, known to have been weaponized successfully in the past. The engineering problems would be known to have a solution, and testing programs could be considerably reduced.

The technical annex also suggested, however, that "[t]he current level of sophistication for many biological agents is low, but there is enormous potential—based on advances in modern molecular biology, fermentation and drug delivery technology—for making more sophisticated weapons" (23). The annex noted that while historically it had been possible to alter the characteristics of biological weapons agents, making one change by ordinary methods often produced a second change—detrimental and unwanted—in another desired factor in the agent's characteristics. Now, however, "[a]dvances in biotechnology, genetic engineering, and related scientific fields provide increasing potential to control more of these factors, possibly leading to the ability to use biological warfare agents as tactical battlefield weapons" (23).

A set of new types of agents that might be produced by genetic engineering was then described:

- Benign microorganisms, genetically altered to produce a toxin, venom, or bioregulator;
- Microorganisms resistant to antibiotics, standard vaccines, and therapeutics;
- Microorganisms with enhanced aerosol and environmental stability.
- Immunologically altered microorganisms able to defeat standard identification, detection, and diagnostic methods;
- Combinations of the above four types with improved delivery systems (23).

For the longer term, the annex suggested four technological trends that would significantly influence the likelihood of new agents being developed:

- Genetically engineered vectors in the form of modified infectious organisms will be increasingly employed as tools in medicine and the techniques become more widely available.
- Strides will be made in understanding infectious disease mechanisms and in microbial genetics that are responsible for disease processes.
- An increased understanding of the human immune system function and disease mechanisms will shed light on the circumstances that cause individual susceptibility to infectious disease.
- Vaccines and antidotes will be improved over the long term, perhaps to the point where classical biological warfare agents will offer less utility as a means of causing casualties (23).

Clearly, our growing understanding of the mechanism of action of disease agents and of our own defensive immune system will have an enormous impact. Such possibilities will be examined in succeeding chapters, but first it must be asked, Why, if toxins and bioregulators are chemicals and are therefore also covered by the new and comprehensive Chemical Weapons Convention, should there be any concern about their potential misuse?

THE CHEMICAL WEAPONS CONVENTION

The Convention on the Prohibition of the Development, Production, Stockpiling, and Use of Chemical Weapons and on Their Destruction (otherwise known as the Chemical Weapons Convention, or CWC) was eventually signed in the early 1990s, after detailed and protracted negotiations during the 1980s (24, 25, 26). It is widely viewed as having many of the attributes needed in a serious arms control treaty. Moreover, it is an equal treaty that gives the same rights and obligations to each of the state parties.

There have, however, been continuing worries over whether the negotiations left a loophole that might allow a new arms race in chemical agents to occur. One analyst concluded a discussion of the problem in the late 1980s by asking his audience not to forget that "the strongest, most effective, most easily verifiable treaty will be one that includes a ban on the use of herbicides and irritants [e.g., tear gas] in war" (27).

There is no doubt that herbicides cannot be used today as they were in Vietnam. The preamble to the CWC states clearly, "[r]ecognising the prohibition, embodied in the pertinent agreements and relevant principles of international law of the use of herbicides as a method of warfare." It is also accepted that riot control agents can only be used domestically in peacetime. The problem arises from the potential utility of riot control–type agents in *warfare*. As one authoritative source noted in 1994, "Some, by no means a majority, of the negotiating states wished to protect possible applications of disabling chemicals that would either go beyond, or might be criticised as going beyond, applications hitherto customary in the hands of domestic police forces" (28).

The latest manifestation of the problem arose during the ratification of the CWC by the U.S. Senate when it imposed a series of conditions: "*Condition 26* requires that the President certify to Congress that the CWC does not restrict the US use of riot control agents (RCAs), including their use against combatants, in three cases" (29).

Although the cases allowed do not permit the kind of use of tear gas for major military purposes that have occurred in the past and that, in World War I, for example, preceded the use of lethal chemical agents, there is unlikely to be a hard and fast distinction in practice. There is a worrying comment attached to a review of this Senate condition to the effect that "[a]s research and development work progresses in the United States on non-lethal alternatives to RCAs, options may become available that remove the potential requirement to choose between using RCAs or deadly force" (29).

In short, despite the existence of the CWC, the search for new chemical agents appears to be continuing in the United States (13). If this is indeed so, similar research and development is probably under way elsewhere in the world as well. There will be a detailed consideration of the verification conditions of the CWC in a later chapter. What needs stressing here is that the convention has apparently not completely eliminated the search for new and more effective chemical agents.

REFERENCES

1. P. Cohen (1998). A terrifying power. *New Scientist* (30 January): 10.
2. E. R. Moxon (1995). Whole genome sequencing of pathogens: A new era in microbiology. *Trends in Microbiology* 3, no. 9: 335–337.
3. M. R. Dando (1999). The development of international legal constraints on biological warfare in the 20th century. In M. Koskenniemi et al., eds., *The Finnish Yearbook of International Law*. Vol. 8. The Hague: Martinus Nijhoff, pp. 1–69.
4. United Nations (1970). *Chemical and Bacteriological (Biological) Weapons and the Effects of Their Possible Use*. New York.
5. World Health Organization (1970). *Health Aspects of Chemical and Biological Weapons*. Geneva.
6. United Nations (1980). Final Declaration of the First Review Conference, BWC/CONF.I/10. Final Declaration of the Second Review Conference, BWC/CONF.II/13/II. In J. Goldblat and T. Bernauer, *The Third Review of the Biological Weapons Convention: Issues and Proposals*. Research Paper No. 9. United Nations Institute for Disarmament Research, Geneva (UNIDIR/91/17), pp. 37–50.
7. United Nations (1980). *New Scientific and Technological Developments Relevant to the Convention on the Prohibition of the Development, Production and Stockpiling of Bacteriological (Biological) and Toxin Weapons and on Their Destruction*. BWC/CONF.I/5, Geneva, 6 February.
8. F. B. Armstrong et al. (1981). *Recombinant DNA and the Biological Warfare Threat*. DPG-S450A, U.S. Army, Dugway Proving Ground, Utah, May.
9. T. Karpetsky, ed. (1986). *Technologic Changes Since 1972: Implications for a Biological Warfare Convention*. CRDC-CR-86017, U.S. Army Chemical Research and Development Center, Aberdeen Proving Ground, Maryland, March.
10. See, for example, National Defense Research Institute (1987). *Genetic Engineering and Biological Weapons,* Umeå, Sweden (translated by the Office of International Affairs, National Technical Information Service, Springfield, Va., May 1988).
11. United Nations (1991). *Background Document on New Scientific and Technological Developments Relevant to the Convention on the Prohibition of the Development, Production and Stockpiling of Bacteriological (Biological) and Toxin Weapons and on Their Destruction*. BWC/CONF.III/4, Geneva, 4 August.

12. Canada (1991). *Novel Toxins and Bioregulators: The Emerging Scientific and Technological Issues Relating to Verification and the Biological and Toxin Weapons Convention.* Ottawa, September.

13. M. R. Dando (1996). *A New Form of Warfare: The Rise of Non-Lethal Weapons.* London: Brassey's.

14. United States Air Force Scientific Advisory Board (1997). *New World Vistas: Air and Space Power for the 21st Century.* Washington, D.C.: United States Air Force.

15. United Nations (1991). *Final Declaration of the Third Review Conference of the Parties to the Convention on the Prohibition of the Development, Production and Stockpiling of Bacteriological (Biological) and Toxin Weapons and on Their Destruction.* BWC/CONF.III/23, Geneva, September.

16. United Nations (1996). *Background Paper on New Scientific and Technological Developments Relevant to the Convention on the Prohibition of the Development, Production and Stockpiling of Bacteriological (Biological) and Toxin Weapons and on Their Destruction.* BWC/CONF.IV/4, Geneva, 30 October.

17. See, for example, B. Dubuis (1994). *Recombinant DNA and Biological Warfare.* IMS 94-10, Institut für militarische Sicherheitstechnik, ETH Zürich, OH-8001 Zurich.

18. V. Nathanson, M. Darvell, and M. R. Dando (1999). *Biotechnology, Weapons and Humanity.* London: Harwood Academic (for the British Medical Association).

19. F. S. Collins et al. (1998). New goals for the U.S. Human Genome Project: 1998–2003. *Science* 282 (23 October): 682–689.

20. United Nations (1996). *Final Declaration of the Fourth Review Conference of the Parties to the Convention on the Prohibition of the Development, Production and Stockpiling of Bacteriological (Biological) and Toxin Weapons and on Their Destruction.* BWC/CONF.IV/9, Geneva, December.

21. J. T. Rifkin (1998). *The Biotech Century: The Coming Age of Genetic Commerce.* London: Victor Gollancz.

22. M. R. Dando (1999). The impact of the development of modern biology and medicine on the evolution of offensive biological warfare programmes in the 20th century. *Defense Analysis* 15, no. 2: 43–62.

23. W. S. Cohen (1997). *Proliferation: Threat and Response.* Technical annex available online at http://www.defenselink.mil/pubs/prolif97/annex.html.

24. For the main text of the convention see, "CW Convention," *Arms Control Today*, April 1997, pp. 15–28.

25. For details of the convention, see A. W. Dorn (1993). *Index to the Chemical Weapons Convention.* UNIDIR Research Paper No. 18. United Nations, New York.

26. For an introduction to the convention, see A. E. Smithson, ed. (1993). *The Chemical Weapons Convention Handbook.* Washington, D.C.: The Henry L. Stimson Center.

27. R. J. McElroy (1989). "Tear gas and herbicides: Their use in warfare and the importance of prohibiting such use." Paper presented to a Conference on Chemical and Biological Disarmament, International Commission of Health Professionals, 24–27 May, Geneva.

28. Editorial (1994). New technologies and a loophole in the convention. *Chemical Weapons Convention Bulletin* 23: 1–2.

29. A. Gordon (1997). Implications of the US resolution of ratification. *The CBW Conventions Bulletin* 28: 1–6.

4

Toxins

In Chapter 2 a differentiation was made between toxins and bioregulators. A poison was defined as a substance that damages health or causes death when introduced into the body of a victim, whereas a toxin was described as a type of poison produced by a living organism. It was suggested that, by definition, a toxin is something that is not a naturally occurring constituent of the body being damaged. It was argued that a bioregulator—which *is* a naturally occurring constituent of a victim's body—could also be misused, to damage health or cause death by introducing unnatural quantities of it into the body. These straightforward definitions should be kept in mind as we briefly review some of the complex issues that must be considered in arms control negotiations. First, it is worth reiterating that many *toxic* chemicals manufactured bear no relationship at all to naturally occurring toxins. Books on the treatment of poisoning have numerous chapters (for instance, on the misuse of designer drugs) other than those dealing with natural toxins such as snake venoms (1). So "all toxins are toxic chemicals but all toxic chemicals are not toxins," as one commentator wrote, after reviewing numerous definitions (2).

In discussions leading up to the agreement of the Biological and Toxin Weapons Convention, Sweden noted in a working paper for the Conference of the Committee on Disarmament in 1971 that the term *toxin* was often used in a vague manner and thus put forward criteria to be used in any proper definition of a toxin (3). Sweden argued that four factors, or sets of factors, had to be considered: the natural origin or occurrence of the compound; the degree of toxicity, type of toxic activity, and mode of action; the chemical nature of the compound; and chemical operations producing toxins and poisonous substances related to toxins (for example, synthetic, semi-synthetic, or chemically modified). The paper added: "The fact that very toxic compounds of biological origin have important use as medical drugs in small quantities must be recognised and provided for in a treaty" (3).

45

A letter to the editor of the journal *Toxicon*, in 1970, suggested that though it was not possible to give a perfect strict definition of a toxin, a substance satisfying the following criteria would meet the definition: It should be a substance of natural occurrence (plant, animal, bacteria, etc.); it should be foreign to the victim; and the compound should be predominantly toxic and adverse to the well-being or life of the victim (4). The complexities were well illustrated by the example of histamine in wasp venom introduced into a human through a sting. Although histamine occurs naturally in humans, the histamine from the sting is nevertheless considered a toxin because it is applied in a toxic dose under unusual conditions. Similarly, digitoxin, the active ingredient in digitalis poisoning, would be considered a toxin even though it might be used for therapeutic purposes, such as to treat heart disease.

NATURAL TOXINS

Despite such complexities, it is not too difficult to recognize a wide range of natural toxins produced by living organisms. One type is snake venom. Injuries and deaths are caused by venomous snakes in most parts of the world, and in the tropics they can be a major health hazard. There are five families of venomous snakes (Table 4.1).

The venoms of such snakes are complex and vary between the different types. Some components of the venom may be dedicated to stopping blood clotting (and thus preventing restriction of the poison to the region of the bite), but other toxins may also be present: "Neurotoxins are found in the venoms of vipers, elapids, and hydrophiids. . . . Textilotoxin, from the Australian brown snake (*Pseudomya textilis*) is the most potent snake venom toxin known" (1).

Some potent toxins are also produced by amphibians. These include bufotoxin from the toad, *Bufo alvarious*, and batrachotoxin from poison-dart

Table 4.1 Families of Venomous Snakes

Family Name	Common Name
Colubridae	Back-fanged, arboreal snakes such as the African boomslang and twig snakes
Elapidae	Cobras, kraits, mambas, coral snakes, and the terrestrial Australian venomous snakes
Hydrophiidae	Sea snakes
Viperidae	Vipers, adders, pit vipers, and rattlesnakes
Atractaspididae	Burrowing asps or stiletto snakes

Source: From reference 1.

frogs such as *Phyllobates terribilis*. One such frog can contain some 1.9 milligrams of the toxin when the lethal dose for a man is between 0.02 and 0.2 milligrams! Curiously, a related toxin, homobatrachotoxin, has been found in three species of birds in New Guinea (5). The infamous toxin of puffer fish, tetrodotoxin, is also found in some species of newts (6).

Many other aquatic animals produce toxins. In the phylum Echinodermata, for example, which includes sea urchins, starfish, and sea cucumbers, "[o]f 6000 species, 80 are venomous to man. The toxins vary in chemistry and modes of action" (1). The molluscan *Conus* species also exhibit an amazing range of conotoxins (7). Among the fish, "[o]ver 200 species, including stingray, scorpion fish, zebra fish, stonefish, weevers, toadfish, stargazers, ratfish, catfish, surgeon fish, and several species of shark, are known to be venomous" (1). These fish are usually slow swimmers with spines or stings containing specialized tissues that secrete a pain-producing toxin as a means of defense.

The dangers from the venom of arthropods such as bees, wasps, ants, scorpions, and spiders have become particularly well known in recent years, partly through the introduction of African bees into Brazil in the mid-1950s. These bees were introduced in an attempt to breed bees better suited to hot climates, but some escaped and formed wild colonies. Worse, these bees tend to attack in large numbers, rather than as individuals, and are therefore more likely to provoke severe allergic reactions in their victims. The bees have also since managed to spread north at an average rate of 200 to 300 miles per year and are now in North America, thus increasing the number of people vulnerable to attack.

Plants, of course, produce a vast range of substances dangerous to humans. These include alkaloids, glycosides, proteins (such as the well-known toxins abrin and ricin), oxalates, resins, and so on. As noted previously, ricin is obtained from the castor bean, *Ricinus communis*. During processing, the castor oil is removed and ricin is left in the remaining fiber, from which it can be easily extracted. Abrin is structurally similar to ricin. It is part of a complex mixture of substances obtainable from the jequirity bean, *Abrus precatorius*. Few people will have difficulty thinking of other poisonous plants like yew, laburnum, poison ivy, and the Christmas favorites mistletoe and holly, and most people are aware of the need to be very careful about eating wild mushrooms unless they are identified as safe by an expert.

Considerable controversy arose in the 1980s when the United States accused the then Soviet Union of actually using trichothecenes (secondary metabolites of fungi that frequently contaminate grain) as chemical warfare agents in Asia (8). This accusation, of the use of so-called yellow rain, did not stand up to scientific analysis. It is nevertheless important to note that these trichothecenes present an unusual threat because they can act percutaneously (through the skin) in a way that most other toxins of concern cannot. It is also clear that these toxins do present a public health hazard and that a great deal more needs to be known about them (9).

Trichothecenes are toxins produced by certain species of fungi such as *Fusarium, Myrothecium, Trichoderma,* and others, and constitute a large enough family of toxins in themselves. However, there are many other fungi that produce mycotoxins with adverse effects on humans (10). As noted earlier, Iraq's offensive biological weapons program included work on aflatoxin, and it has been suggested that mycotoxins, in combination with standard nerve agents, were used by Iraq in its 1984 attack on Iranian troops on Majnoon Island (11, 12).

Despite the profusion of different types of toxins accepted today, a 1981 working paper by the former Czechoslovakia for the Committee on Disarmament pointed out that although the introduction of the term *toxin* was rather obscure, it originated late in the nineteenth century when diphtheria, tetanus, and botulism were shown to cause their lethal effects not directly—that is, by proliferation of the bacteria involved—but indirectly, through buildup of the toxic products they excreted. The paper defined a poison as "any chemical substance which when introduced into a suitable host . . . results in overt damage to tissues or interruption of normal physiological activities" (13). It continued:

> The distinction between poison and toxin was made by early investigators although no hard rules were even established, nor are they established today. A tacit agreement was arrived at, namely that *toxins are antigenic poisons of microbial origin* (the term antigenic means that they are able to induce the antibody response in the body; to be able to do this, their molecules must have rather high molecular weight and a complex structure—in most instances they are *proteins*). (original emphases) (13)

The paper went on to argue the necessity of using a more modern definition that incorporates the much wider range of toxins discussed here rather than just including bacterial toxins. However, there can be no doubting the importance of bacterial toxins in our discussion of the potential misuse of biotechnology.

The Czechoslovakia paper is also of interest because it argued that "toxins are not produced by a micro-organism just to be toxic" but that "they serve as tools necessary mainly for active accommodation of the microenvironment, to create conditions needed for metabolism, growth and proliferation of microbial cells" (13). The point was then illustrated by reference to the enterotoxin produced by the organism responsible for cholera. The enterotoxin reacts with the cells of the intestine and causes them to produce the copious fluid required by the bacteria; this, of course, is the reason for the severe diarrhea experienced by the victim. The mechanisms by which toxins act can thus be rather complex as they are likely to be the result of a long evolutionary interaction between the victim species and the toxin-producing species (14).

CURRENT MILITARY CONCERNS

In 1992, during the meetings of the verification experts (VEREX) set up at the Third Review Conference of the Biological and Toxin Weapons Convention to examine whether it was possible, on a scientific basis, to verify the convention, the Russian Federation produced the *Illustrative List of Potential BW Agents*. This list contained a large number of bacterial, rickettsial, chlamydial, fungal, and viral species, as might be expected. It also contained a small number of neuropeptides (see Chapter 5) and a large number of toxins. A sampling from that list follows:

Toxins of microorganisms: botulinum toxins, enterotoxin A *Staphylococcus aureus,* neurotoxin *Shigella dysenteriae*
Toxins of animal origin: tetrodotoxin, conotoxins, palytoxin, batrachotoxin
Toxins of plants and seaweed toxins: Modeccin, abrin, maitotoxin, brevetoxin, ricin, saxitoxin
Toxins of snakes and spiders: taipoxin, textilotoxin, ammodytoxin, notexin, beta bungarotoxin, alpha-, beta-scorpion toxins, latrotoxin, diamphotoxin
Neuropeptides: endothelin, dermorphin, amilyn (15)

In a footnote to the above list, the authors note that ricin and saxitoxin are named in Schedule 1 of the draft Chemical Weapons Convention, which is the most dangerous category of chemicals.

The Chinese *People's Military Surgeon* of late 1994 set out concerns about the U.S. and Soviet research programs under the title "Development of Contemporary Chemical [and] Biological Weapons and Medical Protection Against Them" (16). It argued, for example, that

America and the former Soviet Union separated venom from marine organisms, snakes, and scorpions to make various kinds of toxins. The toxicity of the toxins of certain . . . organisms is several tens to several hundreds of times stronger than the toxicity of . . . nerve toxicants [agents], and they are difficult for the existing detecting and testing equipment to test. (16)

The article went on to express anxiety about the use of modern biotechnology (genetic engineering) techniques in military studies of these toxins. Though the United States no longer has an offensive biological weapons program, it would be difficult to deny that the U.S. military has long had an interest in toxins and their properties. The United States certainly studied toxins intensively during the period from World War II to the late 1960s when it did have an offensive program (17).

A further indication of the attention being given to toxins by the military today was provided by an article entitled "Toxins: The Emerging Threat," in the specialist publication *ASA Newsletter* in 1998 (18). The author was Murray Hamilton, an expert at the Canadian Defence Research Establishment at Suffield. As the title implied, the article stressed the impact of new technology, particularly the impact of computing capabilities in combination with modern biotechnology. It suggested that "a significant program of new threat (toxin or mid-spectrum) agent development could be undertaken with a very modest outlay of resources (something along the lines of 'virtual' CW development). Furthermore, the research, for the most part, could be done anywhere by a very small team with validation needed only in the final stages" (18).

The use of computing to refine the structure, and thus the function, of chemicals will be discussed further in a later chapter. The question that has to be asked now is whether this toxin threat represents an impossible problem. If there are, in fact, an enormous number of diverse natural toxins and the possibility of using computing and biotechnology to design many more, what hope is there of any kind of defense?

DEFENSE AGAINST TOXIN WEAPONS

Hamilton's article made an interesting comparison between standard nerve agents and toxins such as tetrodotoxin or botulinum toxin. This comparison is set out in Table 4.2. Toxin weapons clearly still have some disadvantages when compared with nerve agents. On the one hand, nerve agents would be easier to produce and weaponize and could act percutaneously against unprotected people. On the other hand, toxins would be more difficult for an enemy to detect, and some would be effective in much smaller quantities (submicrogram lethality).

According to the U.S. Army standard publication *Medical Aspects of Chemical and Biological Warfare,* this issue of the lethality of toxins is the key to turning the threat into a more manageable problem. Most toxins are simply not toxic enough to represent a militarily significant threat in reasonably small quantities. This is an important argument worth considering in more detail. In the chapter entitled "Defense Against Toxin Weapons," a toxin is defined as "[a]ny toxic substance that can be produced by an animal, plant, or microbe. Some toxins can also be produced by molecular

Table 4.2 Some Characteristics of Chemical and Toxin Agents

Characteristic	Nerve Agent (e.g., Soman)	Toxin (e.g., botulinum toxin)
Cheaply manufactured	Yes	No (but potentially yes, using modern methods)
Stability:		
in storage	Yes	Yes
in weapons	Yes	Unknown
during dissemination	Yes	Some
Safe to users (e.g., binary chemicals)	Yes	Some
Persistent	Yes	Yes
Volatile	Yes	No
Detectable	Yes	No or not easily
Therapy	Yes	Supportive
Pretreatment or prophylaxis	Yes	Some (vaccine)
Submicrogram lethality	No	Yes
Time to effect	Predictable: seconds to minutes	Predictable: minutes to hours
Exposure risk	Dermal, oral, inhalation	Inhalation, oral

Source: From reference 18.

biological techniques (protein toxins) or by chemical synthesis (low-molecular-weight toxins)" (19).

The most likely route of attack for soldiers or victims of mass terrorism is considered to be through the lungs as a result of inhaling a respirable aerosol. As the author, David Franz, points out, the lack of an effect through the skin for most toxins considerably complicates the attackers' problem. Moreover, once a toxin has settled out from the air, it is unlikely to be sufficiently disturbed again (for example, by troop movements) to once more become a respirable aerosol. A threat would, of course, remain from contamination of food or water, until the toxin had degraded.

When considering the toxin threat, what is important is the lethality that can be achieved in a respirable aerosol. The toxin has to be producible, storable, and stable in an aerosol *and* possess adequate lethality. The crucial question is how much toxin of a given lethality is required to fill a given volume with a small-particle aerosol. The subject has been investigated in the United States both theoretically, using a mathematical model, and by field testing in the 1960s to check the model. According to Franz, "a toxin with an aerosol toxicity of 0.025 µg/kg would require 80 kg of toxin to cover 100 km^2 with an effective cloud that exposes individuals within the cloud to a dose that would be lethal to approximately 50% of those exposed (LD$_{50}$)" (19).

Some LD_{50} rates taken from Franz's account are shown in Table 4.3. Clearly, botulinum toxin has the level of lethality required for effective use in small quantities, but "for toxins less lethal than botulinum or the staphylococcal enterotoxins, hundreds of kilograms or even tons would be needed to cover an area of 100 km² with an effective aerosol" (19).

So for practical purposes, many toxins can be ignored as potential threats. What *is* important, though, is to recognize and understand the highly lethal toxins, and perhaps the moderately lethal toxins (like ricin), which are easily produced in large quantities. Though many hundreds of the known toxins might be used for assassination, and many tens might be toxic enough to be used in an aerosol in a confined space, only the most highly toxic are of major concern to military forces in regard to large-scale, open-air attack today.

Of course, the calculations of LD_{50} for the various toxins had to be made using a number of assumptions, such as that the LD_{50} for personnel was the same as for the animal subjects used in the tests. The estimates have, however, been checked with more accurate measures since the 1960s and can be considered valid for our purposes. Franz concluded:

Table 4.3   Comparative Lethality of Toxins in Laboratory Mice

Agent	Lethality LD_{50} (µg/kg)[a]	Source
Botulinum toxin	0.001	Bacterium
Shiga toxin	0.002	Bacterium
Tetanus toxin	0.002	Bacterium
Abrin	0.04	Plant
Diphtheria toxin	0.10	Bacterium
Maitotoxin	0.10	Marine dinoflagellate
Palytoxin	0.15	Marine soft coral
Textilotoxin	0.60	Elapid snake
Clostridium perfringens toxins	0.1–5.0	Bacterium
Batrachotoxin	2.0	Arrow-poison frog
a-Conotoxin	5.0	Cone snail
Taipoxin	5.0	Elapid snake
Tetrodotoxin	8.0	Puffer fish
Saxitoxin	10.0 (inhalation 2.0)	Marine dinoflagellate
VX nerve gas (for comparison)	15.0	Chemical agent
Staphylococcus enterotoxin B (Rhesus monkey by aerosol)	27.0 (for incapacitation, 100-fold lower)	Bacterium
T-2 toxin	1,210.0	Fungal mycotoxin

Source: From reference 19.
Note: a. Approximate values drawn from many sources: mainly intraperitoneal or intravenous doses.

An armored or infantry division in the field is not at great risk of exposure to a marine toxin whose toxicity is so low that 80 tonnes is needed to produce a MCBW [Mass Casualty Biological/Toxin Weapon] covering 10 km^2. Most marine toxins are simply too difficult to produce in such quantities. Military leaders on today's battlefield should be concerned first about the most toxic bacterial toxins. (19)

This warning is reinforced by considering the *sources* of the most toxic, the highly toxic, and the moderately toxic of the toxins shown in Table 4.4. From the viewpoint of the military leaders referred to by Franz, of most concern for arms control today are the most toxic *bacterial* toxins. This point is underlined by a brief consideration of the other possible candidates.

Toxins can be categorized in many different ways, one of which is by source. Two other helpful means of categorization are by molecular weight and by mechanism of action. For molecular weight, Franz states that *low-molecular-weight* and *protein* toxins are often used: "Low-molecular-weight toxins are typically less than 1,000 daltons (d), or approximately 10 amino acids, and may be either organic molecules [of a non-peptide nature] or peptides. Protein toxins are proteins generally greater than approximately 10 amino acids" (19). For categorization by mechanism of action, there are two main types: neurotoxins, which directly affect the functioning of the nervous system, typically in a temporary or reversible way; and membrane-damaging toxins, which actually destroy or damage tissues and whose effects are less commonly reversible. However, there is not necessarily any correlation between the molecular weight of a toxin and its mode of action.

Table 4.4   Categorization of Toxins by Toxicity

Source of Toxin	Number of Toxins in Each Category			
	Most Toxic ($LD_{50} < 0.025$ µg/kg)	Highly Toxic (0.025–2.5 µg/kg)	Moderately Toxic (> 2.5 µg/kg)	Total
Bacteria	17	12	> 20	> 49
Plant	—	5	> 31	> 36
Fungi	—	—	> 26	> 26
Marine organisms	—	> 46	> 65	> 111
Snakes	—	8	> 116	> 124
Algae	—	2	> 20	> 22
Insects	—	—	> 22	> 22
Amphibians	—	—	> 5	> 5
Total	17	> 73	> 305	> 395

Source: From reference 19.

The related botulinum toxins (seven in all), as noted earlier, are extremely toxic. They cause death by paralyzing the muscles of the respiratory system. These bacterial protein toxins are not easy to produce, but their lethality is such that large amounts of them would not be needed. They can certainly be turned into an effective, lethal, respirable aerosol. Membrane-damaging bacterial toxins, such as those derived from *Escherichia coli* and *Pseudomonas,* are relatively easy to produce but vary in stability. However, their generally lower toxicity means that they are much less of a military concern.

The seven staphylococcal enterotoxins operate by a very different mechanism involving the immune system. These protein toxins could be produced and probably delivered as respirable aerosols in the amounts necessary to produce incapacitation, as the dose needed is at least 100-fold less than that required for lethality (Table 4.3). Many of the low-molecular-weight marine toxins are either difficult to produce or are insufficiently toxic to be considered for battlefield use. Saxitoxin is one example that will be considered in greater detail later. It is produced by a tiny marine dinoflagellate (a protozoan) and is found in shellfish such as mussels and scallops. Saxitoxin acts directly on the nervous system and acts much faster when inhaled than when ingested. At present, this toxin cannot be easily synthesized nor easily produced from natural sources and so is not yet a major threat.

Although trichothecene mycotoxins from fungi are unusual in that they can act through the skin, their toxicity is too low to present a major military threat even when, as in the case of T-2 (a trichothecene mycotoxin from fungi), they are stable in the environment. Some plant toxins, however, even though of limited toxicity, are easy to produce in large quantities. Franz states that 1 million tons of castor beans are processed annually worldwide to produce castor oil (19). The resulting mash of fiber is 3 to 5 percent ricin. About 1,000 kilograms of the ricin toxin would be sufficient for military use.

Until recently, animal venoms could simply not be obtained in sufficient quantities to be of military utility. Now, though, many of the venoms have been sequenced to determine their structure, and the relevant genes that produce them have been cloned and expressed by molecular biological techniques. Some of the smaller venoms have also been synthesized by chemical means. However, because of the difficulties of production that remain, these toxins are not today of major military concern. That position may change as production of peptides becomes more efficient in the future.

Having looked briefly at the alternatives, bacterial toxins are seen to be the major military concern. Yet because *medical* use of these highly toxic toxins is increasing, and will continue to do so, the arms control solution cannot simply be to ban their production. It is necessary to see why these toxins are of medical interest before considering the difficulties of controlling such dual-use (civil and military) substances.

MECHANISMS OF ACTION

The toxins produced by the *Clostridium* genus of bacteria are some of the most toxic substances known. Most people in the West are protected by immunization against the tetanus toxin produced by *Clostridium tetani;* but because of the relatively low incidence of botulinal food poisoning and the anticipated rate of adverse reactions to vaccination, most Westerners are not routinely protected against the toxins produced by *Clostridium botulinum.* We are therefore susceptible to attack with botulinum toxins, and we know that various countries have worked on weaponizing these toxins since World War II.

Victims of tetanus poisoning present with an easily recognized rigid paralysis. This disease was well described at least as far back as the Middle Ages. It results from contamination of a wound with the tetanus bacterium (which occurs naturally in the environment) and then growth of the bacterial colony in the body and consequent toxin production. Victims of botulism, in contrast, present with a flaccid paralysis. The disease was unknown until modern times, when food preservation became a standard practice. If sterilization of canned food is not carried out properly, spores of the bacterium (which are also naturally present in the environment) can grow in the anaerobic conditions and produce their neurotoxin. If the contaminated food is eaten without adequate heating, the dramatic effects of the toxin quickly become evident. Serious outbreaks in the past quickly led to medical investigations and a growing understanding of the disease and how to prevent it.

However, understanding of the *molecular* mechanisms by which tetanus and botulinum toxins cause their effects grew only slowly until the impact of the revolution in genetic engineering of recent years (20). The genes for tetanus toxin, all seven types of botulinum toxin, and other important toxins have been cloned and sequenced, and the amino acid sequences of the toxins discovered. From this basis, crucial insights into how these toxins function have been obtained.

The fundamental unit of the human body is the cell. This consists of a nucleus containing the genetic material surrounded by cytoplasm where the cell's metabolic functions are carried out, the whole enclosed in a cell membrane. Different cell types, for example, the neurons of the nervous system or the muscle cells, have different functions within the body. Many bacterial protein toxins attack cells in a four-stage process: binding of the free toxin to the wall of the host cell; internalization of the toxin into the main body of the cell (but still surrounded by the host cell membrane); translocation across the host cell membrane; and finally, modification of the host cell's metabolic functions. These toxins have a common structure of an A subunit, which is the effective enzyme causing the toxic effect, and a B subunit, which is concerned with binding to the host cell and penetration. The B subunit varies in different toxins (21). Tetanus toxin and the botulinum toxins are made up of three parts: the active A subunit and a two-part B subunit, which has one part concerned with binding to receptors on the host cell wall and the other with getting the active element (A subunit) across the host cell membrane.

As described at the end of Chapter 2, the neurons of the nervous system are specialized to communicate between themselves by means of the release and reception of chemical transmitters. Tetanus toxin specifically interferes with the inhibitory transmitter acting from the spinal cord interneurons on motor neurons. It blocks the inhibitory transmitter and allows excitation of the muscles by motor neurons to go unchecked, free from the normal inhibition. This causes the rigid paralysis (due to continuous contraction) seen in the peripheral muscles of the limbs. Botulinum toxins, however, affect the excitatory transmitter released from motor neurons at peripheral neuromuscular junctions of the limbs. They block the release of the excitatory transmitter and this leads to the flaccid, uncontracted state of the muscles (22). In the motor neurons affected by botulinum toxins, the excitatory transmitter is acetylcholine, which is packaged in synaptic vesicles on the presynaptic side of the neuromuscular junction (the junction between motor neuron and muscle fiber). Disruption of these vesicles by botulinum toxin has now been studied in considerable detail, and it is now known how, by various enzymatic mechanisms, the toxin produces the overt symptoms of the disease (23). Presumably, the function of the toxin, in evolutionary terms, is to kill the various infected mammalian species so that the bacterium can grow in the anaerobic conditions of their dead bodies and then be distributed into the environment as the bodies decompose. With the clear understanding we now have of the toxin's structure and function, though, it is finding increasing applications in medicine.

One type of medical use is in counteracting disease states characterized by hyperfunction of the cholinergic nerve terminals. As one recent review noted:

> Botulinum toxin (BTX), a purified form of the neurotoxin responsible for botulism, is used worldwide for the treatment of abnormal muscle contractions. The ability of BTX to block acetylcholine release in a long-lasting but reversible fashion with few side effects has made it an important tool in a wide variety of neuromuscular disorders, including the dystonias, tremor, tics and spasticity. (24)

It seems likely that this type of medical use of the toxin will grow, both in areas where it has proved useful over the past twenty years and in new ones. A more sophisticated use of bacterial toxins, however, has resulted from their structural features—an A subunit for the toxic action and various B subunits for cell entry. It has proved possible, in some toxins, to split the two parts of the toxin and to combine the active toxic part (A subunit) with receptors for docking and entry to different types of cells (25). In this way, *chimeric toxins* can be created, with specific affinity for, and damaging action on, specific types of cells. The potential therapeutic uses of such toxins, for example, to target cancer cells, are obvious, and research on chimeric toxins is likely to produce many new ways of using these materials, such as against viral infections (26, 27).

THE DILEMMAS OF DUAL-USE TECHNOLOGY

It is hardly surprising to find widespread civil interest in toxins that might be used for medical purposes, and it is certain to increase as more uses are discovered and developed for these chemicals (28, 29). That interest will surely make the task of preventing the misuse of toxins more difficult. An obvious example of the potential problems arose soon after the entry into force of the Chemical Weapons Convention.

It had been decided to make clear that the CWC covered toxins by placing two, ricin and saxitoxin, on Schedule 1 of the convention. The Schedule 1 designation was intended to apply to chemical weapons and their precursors, that is, to substances that presented the greatest threat to the objectives of the convention. The provisions applied to such chemicals include no export to states not party to the convention; thirty days advance notice to the Organization for the Prohibition of Chemical Weapons of transfers between state parties; and no re-export to a third state party.

Toxins produced by marine animals present health hazards to humans. One of these hazards is paralytic shellfish poisoning caused by saxitoxin. The toxin is produced by a dinoflagellate, *Gonyaulax catanella*, and concentrated in filter-feeding shellfish. When there is a bloom (red tide) of the dinoflagellate, there can be a particularly dangerous buildup of the toxin in the filter-feeding mollusks that can be lethal to people who eat the contaminated shellfish. There is no known antidote to the poison. This type of poisoning occurs unpredictably in different parts of the world and the economic consequences are severe for fisheries affected by it. There is an obvious need for means of monitoring such outbreaks but no means of predicting where this monitoring will be needed next.

A technical seminar held by the OPCW in 1998 examined the problems caused by the fact that the only known assay for saxitoxin involved the use of minute amounts of saxitoxin itself for calibration purposes. Some of the saxitoxin used for the assay had come from Canada, and some, in a tritiated radioactive form, from the United Kingdom, after treatment of material imported into the UK from the United States (30). Among the problems were that the thirty days' prior notification of export of saxitoxin required by the convention prevented that assay system getting to the places where it was needed in good time; and that the UK was not able, under the rules of the convention, to re-export its tritiated saxitoxin to other state parties. Not only that, the regulations were making it very difficult to carry out research involving saxitoxin when it was extremely useful to the scientific community investigating the operation of the nervous system to do so. In this situation, both Canada and the UK had proposed that there should be some temporary solution whereby the regulations could be relaxed pending a longer-term solution. This seemed sensible, particularly as the convention is not supposed to be implemented in such a way as to hamper "international co-operation in the field of chemical activities . . . including the international exchange . . . or use . . . of chemicals . . . for purposes not prohibited under this Convention" (31).

Nevertheless, it took two years of debate (1997–1999) to agree what should be done. State parties were reluctant to accept easily what appeared to be an amendment of the obligations undertaken in the agreement. This, of course, is quite understandable because easy amendment in one case could precipitate requests for many other amendments relating to other "special" circumstances.

FUTURES

In 1997 the U.S. Department of Defense issued a report, *Proliferation: Threat and Response*. This included an interesting technical annex on biological warfare that states: "The current level of sophistication of BW is comparatively low, but there is *enormous potential*—based on advances in modern molecular biology, fermentation and drug delivery technology—for making sophisticated weapons" (emphasis added) (32).

The report listed a series of potential types of novel biological agents (microorganisms) that might be produced through genetic engineering (these were discussed in Chapter 3). The report commented, in part: "With today's much more powerful techniques, infectious organisms can be modified to bring about disease in different ways and to enable relatively benign organisms to cause harmful effects" (32). This nightmarish possibility was unfortunately realized in the massive, illegal, offensive biological weapons program of the former Soviet Union.

It appears that when the Biological and Toxin Weapons Convention was agreed in the early 1970s, the former Soviet Union decided to embark on a massive expansion of its offensive biological weapons program. Because the BTWC had no effective verification measures attached to it, the Soviet Union's illegal program remained hidden from public view until the 1990s, despite the concerns raised by incidents such as the release of anthrax from a military facility in Sverdlovsk in 1979. Information about the program started to enter the public domain as important defectors began speaking openly in the West about what had been done. Perhaps the most complete account yet available has come from Ken Alibek in his book *Biohazard*, published in mid-1999 (33). Alibek gives an autobiographical account of his career from junior officer up through very senior positions and finally his defection to the West.

In one chapter he recounts part of his experience in relation to the Soviet "Project Bonfire." Alibek attended a long, boring review meeting in 1989 at which one of the last speakers was reporting on a rather lengthy and previously unsuccessful attempt to produce a new kind of toxin weapon. Alibek recounts that he was too tired to listen properly as the young scientist began to recount the latest effort to transfer toxic genes into bacteria. Then, he writes: "My attention perked [up] when the scientist announced that a suitable bacterial host had been found for myelin toxin. . . . Lab results had been excellent, and a series of animal experiments had been conducted" (33).

The tests had shown that the animals infected had developed both the disease caused by the bacteria *and* a paralysis resulting from the toxin attacking the myelin sheathing around their nerves. Alibek's account continues: "The test was a success. A single genetically engineered agent had produced symptoms of two different diseases, one of which could not be traced. The room was absolutely silent. We all recognised the implications" (33). They had created a new class of weapon. They could introduce the gene of a toxin or a bioregulator into a microorganism that would then not only manufacture the toxin or bioregulator but also act as a carrier (vector) for transferring the poisonous material to the victim.

Little wonder then that the U.S. Department of Defense suggested that there was "enormous potential" for the development of more sophisticated biological weapons. If we assume that, potentially, the genes for any of the vast range of naturally produced toxins (and their vastly variable effects, by different mechanisms) might be introduced into a variety of environmentally hardy infectious organisms, the long-term future threat from toxin weapons could change quite radically. It would no longer be a case of worrying about the delivery of a relatively small number of reasonably well-characterized bacterial toxins. Imagine the problems for a defender, given even a few of the possible toxins and mechanisms of action that might be encountered. Below are just some of the toxins of concern to the U.S. military in the early 1990s.

> The Biological Defense Research Program (BDRP) is directed against agents of biological origin which are potential military medical threats. . . . Toxins of major interest include:
>
> * blue-green algal toxins (microcystin, anatoxin A);
> * dinoflagellate toxins (saxitoxin, gonyautoxins, brevetoxin, palytoxin);
> * vertebrate toxins (tetrodotoxin, batrachotoxin);
> * protein synthesis inhibiting plant toxins (ricin);
> * protein and peptide toxins of other [than above] biological origin (including pre- and postsynaptic neurotoxins, and membrane active substances);
> * dermally active toxins (lyngbyatoxin).
>
> Physiologically active compounds [bioregulators] of biological origin are also of interest. (34)

In its 1997 technical annex, the U.S. Department of Defense also suggested that there were a number of technological trends that could be important in influencing the development of future kinds of biological weapons (these trends were discussed in Chapter 3). Of particular concern here is the third of these, which suggests that "[a]n increased understanding of the human immune system function and other disease mechanisms will in turn shed light on the circumstances that cause individual susceptibility to disease" (32). So far, offensive biological warfare programs appear to have concentrated on the production of agents to attack a victim's body directly. Another approach, however, would be to destroy the victim's *defenses,* thus increasing susceptibility to attack and vulnerability to opportunistic pathogens in the environment. Destruction of a victim's defenses is, of course, the basis of acquired immune deficiency syndrome (AIDS). The virus causing the disease attacks an important element in the human defense (immune) system.

How then does the body's defense system work, and are there already ways in which a weapons designer might consider attacking it? Many chemicals encountered by humans have been shown to affect the immune system or are suspected of possessing that capability. Well-known examples are the drugs used to suppress the operation of the immune system after an organ transplant operation. If the immune system is not suppressed after this type of surgery, the new (foreign) tissue will be recognized as such and rejected. Other substances have been found to increase the activity of the immune system or to cause the immune system to attack the body itself (autoimmunity). The inadvertent introduction of immunotoxic chemicals into the environment in industrial operations is obviously a cause of considerable concern to governments (35).

The immune system has two components in humans. One of these, the *innate* immune system, is nonspecific and appears to be ancient in evolutionary terms (36). It provides mechanical barriers to the entry of pathogens (for example, the skin) and bactericidal substances that are activated when bacteria do enter the body. The second part of the immune system is highly specific, adaptive, and very complex. It is concerned with *acquired* immunity. This second, specific, part of the system has two responses: "*humoral* and *cell-mediated,* which develop in parallel. . . . Humoral immunity depends on the appearance in the blood of antibodies produced by plasma cells. . . . Cell-mediated immunity depends mainly on the development of T cells that are specifically responsive to the inducing agent" (37).

The cross-links between humoral and cell-mediated immunity are complex but depend, in part, on the activity of particular biologically active peptides called cytokines. The plasma cells that secrete antibodies into the blood are called B cells. However, "[m]any antigens do not stimulate antibody production without the help of T lymphocytes. These antigens first bind to the B cell, which must then be exposed to T cell–derived lymphokines [a form of cytokine], i.e. helper factors, before the antibody can be produced" (37). Of interest here is how the T cell–derived lymphokines are activated.

Some immune system cells that digest foreign material have a special protein called major histocompatibility complex class II (MHC II) that is able to present fragments of the foreign material as peptides on the outside of the cell. Receptors on the T cells recognize and lock onto these presented peptides, and only then do the T cells begin to divide and secrete the lymphokines that, in turn, stimulate the B cells. Though this is only a part of a complex interactive system in which B cells can also stimulate T cells, this MHC II/T cell interaction is an important amplifying element in the immune response (38).

In the late 1980s and early 1990s it was shown that staphylococcal enterotoxins have the ability to subvert this system (39). Instead of the T cell being activated by binding onto the MHC II–presented peptide in the normal way, staphylococcal enterotoxin B, for example, was able to lock onto and bind the T cell receptor (TCR) together with the MHC II protein at points differing from those on the highly variable portion of the MHC II protein, as in the normal response. The toxin actually binds to the conserved (V_β) chains in the TCR (Figure 4.1). As one recent review noted, molecules like SEB "specifically activate . . . those T cells that express particular V_β chains in the TCR, binding to these chains with high affinity. These molecules activate larger numbers of T cells than processed antigens [the fragments of molecules in the normal response] and, as a consequence, are called superantigens" (40). The overproduction of cytokines resulting

Figure 4.1   Diagrammatic Cross-Section of the Interaction Between Superantigen and MHC Class II and the TCR Complex

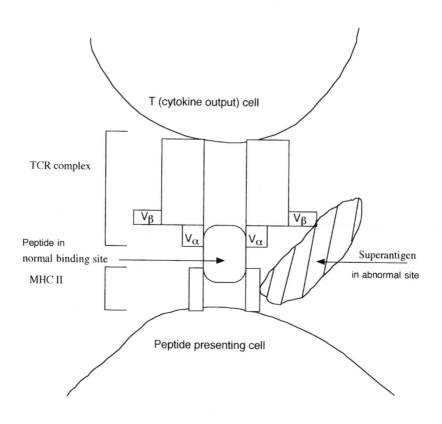

from this over-stimulation of the T cells of the immune system is thought to be the main reason for most of the ill-effects of SEB, although the mechanism is undoubtedly complex (41, 42).

So, although unaware of it at the time, the weapons designers who weaponized SEB in the mid-twentieth century were *already* using a weapon that exerted its effects by attacking the human immune system! We still have much to learn about the role of superantigens, and new knowledge derived from further study will almost certainly open up new ways in which weapons could be designed (43).

The main bearing of the information presented in this chapter is that, though present concerns must center on the classical agents like botulinum toxins—weaponized in mid-twentieth-century offensive biological weapons programs—there will be many new ways in which toxins might be misused in new biological weapons in the twenty-first century. At the same time, the diversity and amounts of toxins used in peaceful civil applications will increase and thus complicate the problem of controlling misuse of these chemicals. In Chapter 5 the misuse of peptides will be examined.

REFERENCES

1. M. J. Ellenhorn et al. (1997). *Ellenhorn's Medical Toxicology: Diagnosis and Treatment of Human Poisoning.* 2d ed. Baltimore: Williams and Wilkins.
2. K. A. Hooton (1990). Letter: Wrong definition. *Chemistry in Britain* (January): 25.
3. Sweden (1971). "Working paper on aspects of the definition of 'toxins.'" Conference of the Committee on Disarmament. CCD/333, 6 July, Geneva.
4. W. Vogt (1970). Letter to the editor: What is a toxin? *Toxicon* 8: 251.
5. J. P. Dumbacher et al. (1992). Homobatrachotoxin in the genus *Pitohui:* Chemical defence in birds? *Science* 258 (30 October): 799–801.
6. N. Saunders (1986). Law and order in the land of the living dead. *New Scientist* 7 (August): 47.
7. S. Wonnacott and F. Dajas (1994). Neurotoxins: Nature's untapped bounty. *TiPS* 15 (January): 1–3.
8. A. Ciegler (1986). Mycotoxins: A new class of chemical weapons. *NBC Defense and Technology International* (April): 52–57.
9. Committee on Protection Against Mycotoxins (1983). *Protection Against Trichothecene Mycotoxins.* Washington, D.C.: National Academy Press.
10. H. B. Schiefer (1983). *Mycotoxicoses: A Summary of Pertinent Facts.* Toxicology Research Centre, University of Saskatchewan, Canada.
11. M. Walderhaug (1998). Aflatoxins: Adaptation of a page from the *FDA Bad Bug Book.* Available online at http://www.geog.umd.edu/EdRes/College... ant_biology/Medicinals/aflatoxin.html.
12. H. Kadivar and S. C. Adams (1991). Treatment of chemical and biological warfare injuries: Insights derived from the 1984 Iraqi attack on Majnoon Island. *Military Medicine* 156 (April): 171–177.
13. Czechoslovakia (1981). *Definition and Characteristics of Toxins.* Committee on Disarmament. CD/199, 24 July, Geneva.
14. P. Singleton (1997). *Bacteria: In Biology, Biotechnology and Medicine.* Chichester: John Wiley and Sons.
15. Russian Federation (1992). *Illustrative List of Potential BW Agents.* Ad Hoc Group of Governmental Experts to Identify and Examine Potential Verification Measures from a Scientific and Technical Standpoint. BWC/CONF.III/VEREX/WP.23, 7 April, Geneva.
16. Guang Chang (1994). Development of contemporary chemical [and] biological weapons and medical protection against them. Part 1 of 2 parts. *People's Military Surgeon* 11 (28 November): 4–8. (Original in Chinese; translated in FBIS-CH 1-95-042, 3 March 1995, pp. 34–35.)
17. F. E. Russell and P. R. Saunders (1967). *Animal Toxins: Proceedings of the First International Symposium on Animal Toxins.* London: Pergamon Press.
18. M. G. Hamilton (1998). Toxins: The emerging threat. *ASA Newsletter* 98, no. 3: 1, 20–25.
19. D. R. Franz (1997). Defense against toxin weapons. In F. R. Sidell et al., eds., *Textbook of Military Medicine, Part I: Medical Aspects of Chemical and*

Biological Warfare. Washington, D.C.: Office of the Surgeon General, Department of the Army, pp. 603–620.

20. E. Marshall (1993). Toxicology goes molecular: Special report. *Science* 259, no. 5 (March): 1394–1398.

21. C. Montecucco and E. Papini (1995). Cell penetration by bacterial protein toxins. *Trends in Microbiology* 3, no. 5: 165–167.

22. P. R. Murray et al. (1998). *Medical Microbiology.* 3d ed. St. Louis, Mo.: Mosby.

23. R. Pellizzari et al. (1999). Tetanus and botulinum neurotoxins: Mechanism of action and therapeutic uses. *Philosophical Transactions of the Royal Society, Series B* 354, no. 1381: 259–268.

24. J. Jankovic and M. F. Brin (1997). Botulinum toxin: Historical perspective and potential new indications. *Muscle and Nerve* (Supplement) 6: S129–145.

25. I. Paston et al. (1992). Recombinant toxins as novel therapeutic agents. *Annual Review of Biochemistry* 61: 331–354.

26. Y. Reiter and I. Paston (1998). Recombinant Fv immunotoxins and Fv fragments as novel agents for cancer therapy and diagnosis. *Trends in Biotechnology* 16, no. 12: 513–520.

27. A. Loregian et al. (1999). Intranuclear delivery of an antiviral peptide mediated by the B subunit of *Escherichia coli* heat-labile enterotoxin. *Proceedings of the National Academy of Sciences USA* 96: 5221–5226.

28. R. McKie (1997). Killer frogs come to the aid of mankind. *The Observer,* 27 April, p. 17.

29. A. L. Harvey (1999). Deadly remedies. *Biologist* 46, no. 3: 102–104.

30. Technical Secretariat (1998). *Technical Seminar on Saxitoxin.* S/78/98. OPCW, 6 October, The Hague.

31. UK (1998). *Saxitoxin: A Cautionary Tale.* EC-X/NAT.1, OPCW, Executive Council, 15 June, The Hague.

32. W. Cohen (1997). *Proliferation: Threat and Response.* Washington, D.C.: U.S. Department of Defense. Available online at http://www.defenselink.mil/pubs/prolif97/index.html.

33. K. Alibek and S. Handeman (1999). *Biohazard.* New York: Random House.

34. Medical Research and Development Command (1991). Press release. U.S. Army, Washington, D.C., January.

35. Office of Technology Assessment (1991). *Identifying and Controlling Immunotoxic Substances: Background Paper.* OTA-BP-BA-75, April (Washington, D.C.: GPO).

36. J. A. Hoffman et al. (1999). Phylogenetic perspectives in innate immunity. *Science* 284 (21 May): 1313–1318.

37. J. Stewart and D. Weir (1997). Innate and acquired immunity. In D. Greenwood et al., eds., *Medical Microbiology.* 15th ed. Edinburgh: Churchill Livingstone.

38. G. J. V. Nassal (1993). Life, death and the immune system. *Scientific American,* September, pp. 21–30.

39. P. Marrack and J. Kappler (1990). The staphylococcal enterotoxins and their relatives. *Science* 248 (11 May): 705–711.

40. C. A. Michie and J. Cohen (1998). The clinical significance of T-cell superantigens. *Trends in Microbiology* 6, no. 2: 61–65.

41. D. Franz et al. (1997). Clinical recognition and management of patients exposed to biological warfare agents. *Journal of the American Medical Association* 278, no. 5: 399–411.

42. C. Weng et al. (1997). Immediate response of leukocytes, cytokines and glucocorticoid hormones in the blood circulation of monkeys following challenge with aerosolized staphylococcal enterotoxin B. *International Immunology* 9, no. 12: 1825–1836.

43. J. Schiffenbauer et al. (1998). The possible role of bacterial superantigens in the pathogenesis of autoimmune disorders. *Immunology Today* 19, no. 3: 117–120.

5

Bioregulatory Peptides

Table 1.1 gave the standard account of the spectrum of chemical and biological agents. Here the possible misuse of perhaps the least well known of these agents, the bioregulatory peptides, is considered. It will be recalled that these are natural substances that could cause illness if administered in abnormal amounts. A hypothetical scenario of such misuse of these *midspectrum* agents was given by Canadian defense analyst Murray Hamilton as part of his review of the emerging threat that was discussed in Chapter 4 (1). Hamilton's article began with a fictitious morning newspaper report: "Montreal, Canada. . . . Officials today are at a loss to explain the attack yesterday that left eight dead and hundreds hospitalized after an apparent exposure to a biological agent in the crowded Place de Congres" (1).

The agent had apparently been disseminated through the ventilation system of the huge building. The account continued: "The casualties are suffering from what appear to be massive cardiovascular problems, but physicians are at a loss for an explanation" (1). No causative organisms were found, but "[c]ardiovascular problems include high blood pressure, heart attacks, stroke, aneurysms and other types of unexplained bleeding" (1).

The journalist argued that, without the effective modern treatment available in a major city, the casualties and deaths could have been much greater. Even in Montreal, the account pointed out, in the absence of an identified specific causative organism, medical treatment was limited to dealing with the symptoms. All that could be established, the story went, was that during the lunch period, when the underground concourse was particularly crowded, some people had noticed a faint smoke or fog about fifteen to thirty minutes before they began to feel ill. Medical staff suggested it was fortunate that the causative agent, whatever it was, had apparently been delivered in a relatively low dosage. Therefore, they had not been totally overwhelmed by the numbers of people requiring intensive care.

At the end of his review of the emerging threat, Hamilton returned to this opening imaginary scenario. The toxic material of this fictitious account had been identified within a couple of days by a special team from the Department of National Defence (DND): "'The poison used was a chemical derived from the venom of a snake' said a senior DND official. 'It is related to a compound produced by our own bodies, which is why it is so potent and specific'" (1). The official pointed out that once the particular class of chemical had been identified, it was possible to use commonly available blood pressure medications to treat the casualties. So much for the fictional account.

Although Hamilton did not name the specific chemical used in his fictitious account, his table of *real* potential threats contains one obvious candidate—sarafotoxin/endothelin. The extract from Hamilton's data for this chemical is shown in Table 5.1. So what we are dealing with here is a chemical—found in human endothelial cells (which line blood vessels) and, in a very slightly different form, in a snake venom—which has specific actions on human smooth muscle at relatively low concentrations. Such smooth muscle occurs in the walls of many internal organs including blood vessels. Sarafotoxin/endothelin may not be the chemical Hamilton had in mind for his imaginary scenario, but it certainly seems worthy of further investigation here, particularly because endothelin was one of three specific neuropeptides mentioned in the Russian Federation's illustrative list of potential biological warfare agents referred to in Chapter 4 (2).

Increasing official concerns about misuse of bioregulatory peptides were discussed in Chapter 3, but it is worth restating what is identified as the threat to people from these agents. In 1988, the journal *New Scientist* quoted the then director of Britain's Chemical Defence Establishment at Porton Down thus: "Bioregulators are substances that are produced naturally in the human body as part of its metabolism" (3). He continued: "[W]hen introduced in an unnatural way they can induce a variety of adverse affects, such as change to blood pressure, pain, sleep and even death. New techniques in biotechnology can synthesise such agents cheaply and in large quantities" (3). A recent U.S. document, *The Biological Chemical Warfare Threat*, makes the same serious points:

Table 5.1   Endothelin/Sarafotoxin

Toxin/Chemical	Source	Category	Mechanism of Action	Target System	Toxicity LD_{50} (µg/kg)
Endothelin (sarafotoxin)	Human endothelial cells (snake venom)	Bioregulator/ toxin	Ca2+ channel activator (indirect)	Smooth/ vascular muscle	60 (in mice)

Source: From reference 1.

Bioregulators are natural substances produced in very small quantities that are essential for normal physiological functioning of the body. They control cell and body physiological functions and regulate a broad range of functions, such as bronchoconstriction, vasodilation, muscle contraction, blood pressure, heart rate, temperature, and immune responses. . . .

These substances can be harmful, however, in large concentrations or if modifications to them bring about changes in the nature and duration of their action. Exploited in such a way for military purposes, they could potentially cause such effects as rapid unconsciousness, heart failure, paralysis, hypotension or hypertension, or psychological disturbances. (4)

A Swedish information document, *Biological Warfare,* reiterated in its chapter on new threats following advances in biotechnology the importance of such bioregulators: "Another field that is rapidly attracting increasing interest is body substances that affect different physiological and biochemical processes within the body. These substances, bioregulators, can generally be regarded as being signal substances that control in one way or another the cell's living processes" (5). In military terms, however, the document points out:

[W]e are dealing with extremely small quantities of these substances that exert their effects in fractions of a second. Possible bioregulatory weapons might be substances that cause pain, that affect blood pressure, or substances that cause drowsiness or sleep. . . .

By means of modern genetic engineering, it is possible to allow bacteria or viruses to produce the substances on a large scale or to use microorganisms in order to spread these substances to humans, plants or animals. (5)

There can be little doubt then that this threat, hardly known to the general public, has to be taken extremely seriously by the security studies community. It is true, as we have seen in Chapter 2, that bioregulatory agents have long been of interest to the military, both for attacking plants and human beings (6). There was obviously concern in the West, during the later stages of the Cold War, that the former Soviet Union might have made major advances in weaponizing such agents (7, 8). What has clearly happened in recent years is that many more of these substances have been discovered, and their mechanisms of action are now being elucidated. Beginning with endothelin, we will discuss some specific examples before returning to the general problem.

ENDOTHELIN

A recent review of current knowledge about endothelin pointed out that, until a few years ago, the vascular endothelium was thought to function merely as a passive barrier to the transfer of various substances such as nutrients. Now it is recognized that this endothelial tissue is, in fact, a widely dispersed "organ system" that plays a role in many physiologically important functions. "Another milestone discovery, made in the mid-1980s, was that the endothelial cell also releases a peptidergic factor that is the most potent and long-lasting endogenous vasoconstrictor yet described" (9). It was rapidly determined that "[t]he activity of this factor was . . . attributed to the 21-amino acid peptide, endothelin" (9). This peptide has a quite unusual structure that, curiously, closely resembles the sarafotoxins found in snake venoms.

The endothelins (ETs) are defined as "21-amino-acid peptides made by epithelial cells that share sequence homologies and biological properties with sarafotoxins. Various isoforms (all with disulfide bonds that link cysteine moieties at positions 1–15 and 3–11) have been identified" (10). There appear to be three types of endothelin (ET-1, ET-2, and ET-3), each of which is controlled by a separate gene and expressed in different tissues. ET-1 is considered to be the most potent vasoconstrictor of the three.

To understand the importance of such peptides, we need to see how they are produced in the body. In simple terms, the nucleotide sequence of the DNA in the genes dictates the complementary sequence of nucleotides in ribonucleic acid (RNA) through a process of transcription, and then the RNA nucleotide sequence dictates the sequence of amino acids in the relevant peptide through a process of translation. A peptide therefore is a chemical composed of a series of amino acids that are specified by a particular gene. The different amino acids, however, do not have identical chemical forms and properties. The *sequence* of amino acids in a peptide is crucial. The *function* of the peptide depends on its final *structural form,* and the sequence of amino acids in a peptide dictates the way the peptide chain *achieves* its final structural form, because of the interaction between the different types of amino acids located in different parts of the chain.

Thus, the sequence of *nucleotides* coded in the DNA of the gene for endothelin-1 ultimately dictates the sequence of amino acids and therefore the final structural form of this peptide. Sometimes, a variation in the sequence of amino acids in a peptide will have little consequence. It will not greatly affect the final structure of the peptide and will have little affect on its function. Sometimes, though, a change in the sequence of amino acids will have subtle effects, and sometimes even a single amino acid change will prevent the peptide from functioning at all. The amino acid sequence of endothelin-1 is shown in Figure 5.1. Endothelin-2 and endothelin-3 have similar sequences and, crucially, share the cysteine-cysteine disulfide bonds at positions 1–15 and 3–11 (11). Moreover, the endothelin-1 of a number of mammalian species share the same general structure.

The first characterization of an endothelin structure was made by showing that cultures of pig endothelial cells produced a substance that

Figure 5.1 Amino Acid Sequence of Endothelin-1

Endothelin-1: molecular weight 2491.9
(bovine, canine, human, mouse, porcine, rat)

Cysteine (1)—serine—*cysteine*—serine—serine—leucine—methionine—aspartic acid—
lysine—glutamic acid—*cysteine*—valine—tyrosine—phenylalanine—*cysteine*—histidine—
leucine—aspartic acid—isoleucine—isoleucine—tryptophan (21)

Cysteine (1) links to cysteine (15), cysteine (3) links to cysteine (11). See Figure 5.2

Source: From reference 11.

could be collected from the surrounding liquid and used to produce contractions in strips of tissue from pig coronary artery. The chemical causing this effect was then isolated and its chemical structure determined. The investigators produced a diagram showing the endothelin as a loop. As can be seen in Figure 5.2, the smaller arm of the loop started at the first cysteine and the structure then bent so that cysteine (3) could connect with cysteine (11) and cysteine (1) with cysteine (15) of the longer arm.

The investigators commented: "The endothelin-type structure with multiple disulphide bonds within a single, relatively short peptide chain is previously unknown among bioactive peptides of mammalian origin" (12). But they noted that similar kinds of structures are found in some toxic peptides in conotoxins from sea snails and neurotoxins in scorpion venoms. Also in the same year, 1988, it was shown that the venom of the burrowing asp, *Atractaspis engaddensis*, contains sarafotoxins that, although they differ in some amino acids in the sequence, are again very similar to endothelin and, in particular, are characterized by having the linked cysteines at positions 1, 3, 11, and 15 (13). Not surprisingly, given the structural similarity, abnormal amounts of these peptides were found to be lethal to mice and, in lower concentrations, to affect heart function in living, intact mice and in isolated rat-heart preparations. As one recent review noted, "[t]he endothelin peptide family consists of the 21 amino-acid isoforms endothelin-1, endothelin-2, endothelin-3, and sarafotoxin (a snake venom)" (14).

Given the prevalence of heart disease in the developed world, these discoveries quickly provoked many other investigations. The three genes for the human endothelins were quickly cloned, and the way in which each was produced from an initially larger peptide was analyzed. It was shown that the nucleotide sequences encoding the three ET peptides were highly conserved, but the preceding and following sequences were much more variable. This led the investigators to suggest that "although the three genes are evolutionarily relatively distant from each other, the genes evolved from the common ancestral gene under a strong pressure to preserve mature endothelin sequences" (15). This strongly indicates the importance

Figure 5.2 Diagrammatic Representation of the Structure of Endothelin

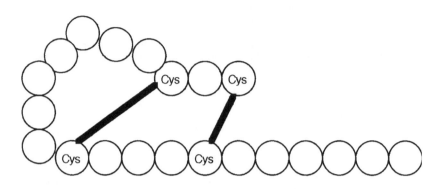

The loop structure of endothelin is shown with
the links between the two sets of cysteine amino acids.

of endothelin in the life of individuals of many species today. If a sequence is strongly conserved during evolution—that is to say, it remains virtually unaltered in a range of mammalian species—it suggests that any mutations that occurred naturally were eliminated because the sequence was required to be in a particular form for vital life functions.

A recent major review concluded that the three endothelin genes are expressed, and the endothelins are thus present, in a wide variety of cell types. The pharmacological responses to endothelin can be divided into two groups. These are mediated by two different types of receptors on the surface of the cells involved. These receptors are termed ET_A and ET_B. Hence, we are dealing with a complex system in which there are three types of endothelins and two types of receptors, all of which suggests that the endothelins may have roles in other complex regulatory systems besides those concerned with the heart and blood vessels.

There will be a detailed discussion in the next two chapters of the importance of different types of receptors and how they might be specifically targeted to a malign effect. For now we should note that in the quest for knowledge with which to solve health problems, an important goal has been to find substances that mimic the effects of endothelins (agonists) or that oppose their effects (antagonists) by operating on the same receptor systems: "Development of potent endothelin receptor agonists and antagonists has provided evidence for the involvement of endothelins in the etiology and pathology of cardiovascular diseases, including chronic heart failure, hypertension, cerebral vasospasm, and pulmonary hypertension" (16). Currently, some of these man-made chemicals are moving from the research stage into clinical trials, and the pace of research remains extremely rapid (17, 18). This short review of the remarkable story of the endothelin family indicates several points worth noting by the security studies community. First, this important set of substances was discovered as recently as the 1980s, and it came about within an area of intense medical interest and study—heart disease. Second, the amazing rate of development of scientific knowledge has to be acknowledged. Since the early 1990s, the medical community has advanced from determining the structure of endothelin to clinical trials of specifically designed medication. Third is the dual-use nature of this science and technology. We know that in the early 1990s the Russian Federation had already signaled its concern over this family of chemicals in an official document for the verification experts process, and in the late 1990s a fictitious scenario that seemed to suggest its use for malign terrorist purposes was being discussed in the technical literature (1).

However, though endothelin/sarafotoxin is a bioregulatory peptide system that could *perhaps* be misused, one hypothetical scenario in the literature is not enough to indicate that these agents pose the same level of threat as toxins. Are there other examples, say, of something different, like an incapacitating agent rather than a lethal agent as endothelin appears to be?

SUBSTANCE P

An article of particular relevance to that question appeared in an applied toxicology journal in mid-1998. As the authors indicated, "[t]he aim of the study was to determine the acute toxicity and the effects on respiration of Substance P (SP), *a possible future warfare agent,* in guinea pigs when the substance was inhaled as an aerosol" (emphasis added) (19). Substance P was co-administered with thiorphan, a chemical that inhibits the action of enzymes that could break down a peptide like Substance P in the body. The authors of the study were from the Defence Research Establishment, Division of Nuclear, Biological, and Chemical Defence in Sweden and were clearly involved in investigating defense against a potential biological warfare agent.

The study demonstrated that administration of Substance P to the conscious animals in this way caused an initial increase in respiratory rate and then a decrease in tidal volume. As exposure to the agent continued, "a decrease in both respiratory rate and further decreases in tidal volume were observed. . . . The decreases in respiratory rate and tidal volume were probably due to bronchoconstriction caused by SP" (19).

Substance P is known to cause contraction of the bronchial smooth muscles in the lung. The authors of the study concluded from their work that Substance P, in combination with thiorphan, produced an extremely potent and toxic aerosol and that "[e]xposure to the substance at extremely low air concentrations may result in incapacitation in humans" (19). It seems clear, then, that Swedish concern was primarily with the potential use of Substance P as an incapacitant. However, the broader story of Substance P has another important message in regard to the development of bioregulators as weapons of war.

Unlike endothelin, which was discovered so recently, the story of Substance P dates from the early 1930s. Work at that time showed that an extract from horse intestine had a hypotensive (blood-pressure-lowering) and spasmogenic activity that differed from the then recently discovered neurotransmitter acetylcholine (20). The active component was named Substance P (the P was short for "preparation"), and it appeared to be a protein or peptide. For the next three decades research remained focused on the chemical properties, pharmacological activities, and tissue distribution of Substance P.

In 1949 a substance with rather similar properties to Substance P was found to be present in high concentration in the posterior salivary gland of an octopus. Despite the difficulty of doing so then, in the early 1960s, the amino acid sequence of this new substance, eledoisin, was determined. Another similar substance, physalaemin, was found in the skin of a South American frog, and it, too, was purified and sequenced. Because these substances had a fast onset of action on gut tissues (compared with slower-acting bradykinins), they were called *tachykinins*. As a consequence of the sequencing, synthetic chemicals closely similar to the tachykinins could now be prepared and tested, and it was suggested that what was vital for their biological activity was a short conserved sequence at one end of the peptide chain. By 1985 there were ten tachykinins described for amphibian species (frogs, toads, etc.), and by 1993 there were twenty-two.

In the late 1960s a peptide was found in cow hypothalamus (part of the brain) that, when purified and sequenced, was recognized as Substance P. The substance was shown to be identical to that obtained by using the original methods of the early 1930s. By this time, however, it was possible to produce pure synthetic Substance P once the structure had been determined. There was a consequent explosion of work. In the late 1970s this area of research was, by one estimate, the third most active in the whole of the life sciences. It became apparent that the defining feature of the tachykinin group was "the highly conserved carboxy-terminal sequence Phe-X-Gly-Leu-Met. . . . To a first approximation, most of the biological activities of the tachykinins depend on this defining sequence" (20).

The amino acids abbreviated in the sequence are as follows: Phe—phenylalanine; Gly—glycine; Leu—leucine; and Met—methionine. A major determinant of the specific activity of a particular tachykinin, however, is the nature of the amino acid at the position denoted by "X" in the above quote. The particular sequence of Substance P is shown in Figure 5.3. It will immediately be evident that Substance P is a very short peptide of eleven amino acids only. There is one difference in the sequence for birds and reptiles as compared with mammals (at position 3), but the conserved terminal section is obvious in both types.

Comparing this account of Substance P with that for endothelin, we see that modern methods give us much greater capabilities for discovering and analyzing such bioregulators. What took decades from 1930 for Substance P was done within ten years for endothelin. As if to underline the point, in the early 1980s it was discovered that Substance P was not the only tachykinin in *mammalian* tissues.

Substance P is a type of neurokinin. Neurokinins are

tachykinin type peptides released by neurons and other cell types, including Substance P, neurokinins a and b (also known under different names), and amphibian peptides such as physalaemin [which all share] a common C-terminal Phe-X-Gly-Leu-Met . . . sequence. Very low concentrations rapidly exert influences on neurons, smooth muscle and vascular permeability. (10)

The variety of receptor types on cells through which these peptides exert their influence will be discussed in the next chapter; but how does aerosolized Substance P cause the constriction of the bronchial muscles of the lung, thus reducing the amount of air available? The fact that inhalation of Substance P causes, first, an increase in respiratory rate and then a decrease in tidal volume suggests a complex mechanism. Certainly, the mechanism indicated by the Swedish authors involves a number of factors (19). It is not necessary to detail all of these, only to note that the authors see part of the action being a direct bronchoconstriction caused by the response of the smooth muscles to Substance P. Another part of the mechanism is the result of Substance P causing histamine to be released. This, in turn, stimulates sensory nerve fibers (C fibers, which convey pain signals) in the lung, input from which brings about a reflex action by the central nervous system. In part, the reflex response causes acetylcholine to be

---

Figure 5.3 Amino Acid Sequence of Substance P

---

1. Avian, reptilian SP: molecular weight 1375.6
arginine—proline—arginine—proline—glutamine—glutamine—phenylalanine—
phenylalanine—glycine—leucine—methionine

2. Mammalian SP: molecular weight 1347.6
arginine—proline—lysine—proline—glutamine—glutamine—phenylalanine—
phenylalanine—glycine—leucine—methionine

Source: From reference 11.

released onto the lung muscles from motor neurons, and this, too, increases bronchoconstriction. Interestingly, Substance P also operates naturally as one of the chemical neurotransmitters that pass input from the C fibers on to neurons in the central nervous system. The latest evidence suggests that glutamate is the transmitter in operation when the pain stimulus is mild and that Substance P also operates when the pain stimulus is moderate to intense (21). However, even in regard to the transmitter function of Substance P, its full role is almost certainly much more complex, involving, for example, long-term stress adaptation and aggressive behavior (22).

This level of complexity in regard to just one bioregulator, Substance P, suggests the necessity of briefly reviewing the topic of chemical bioregulators before turning to the fullest analysis of the role such agents might play in biological warfare. That analysis was carried out on behalf of the Canadian government for the Third Review Conference of the BTWC in 1991 (23).

NEUROPEPTIDES IN GENERAL

The most appropriate way to think about these bioregulators from a scientific viewpoint is to consider them an aspect of the chemical control system of the body and, in particular, of the nervous system. Most nerve cells pass information on to other nerve cells by releasing specialized neurotransmitter chemicals. Acetylcholine was the first such transmitter to be discovered—in the early part of the twentieth century. Other examples are glutamate and dopamine. Most of the earliest described neurotransmitters are not peptides. It was initially supposed that any one nerve cell would use only one neurotransmitter, but it has now been discovered that one nerve cell can employ more than one chemical transmitter. As discovered for C pain-sensory fibers, the second transmitter is often a (neuro)peptide like Substance P.

The overall situation, however, is far more complex because the nervous system—in which rapidly acting nerve cells communicate with one another via chemical neurotransmitters over very short distances—is only one of the body's chemical messenger systems. The second system is the *endocrine* system. This is a slower-acting system in which chemical hormones act generally over greater distances than that between one nerve cell and the next. There is also a third system, the *immune* system, as mentioned in Chapter 4. In this third system, chemical messengers such as cytokines, for example, released by superantigens such as SEB, can mediate profound responses. These three systems—nervous, endocrine, immune—also interact in complex and not-yet-well-understood ways. This has led to the introduction of terms such as "neuroimmunomodulation" to describe the interactions between them (24).

In general, this level of complexity need not concern us too much; but because weapons designers are seeking something whose effects can be simply and reliably reproduced, we can recognize a few points that will help in examining the Canadian account. First, as we saw for Substance P, many of the neuropeptides of interest—because of their action in the fast (nervous) system—were actually first discovered in other organ systems such as the intestine. They were often named in relation to the place they were first discovered, and this name was frequently retained, so the terminology for the neuropeptides is not at all systematic (25). Second, any one neuropeptide can play different roles in different cell types and organ systems. It will become apparent in the next chapter that the recent work on receptor types and subtypes, made possible by the advent of molecular biology, has provided important insights into how the different responses are generated and how they might be manipulated. Third, the human body is an extremely complex system in which effective regulation has evolved with many different feedback and fail-safe systems for any one particular function. Therefore, not only does any single neuropeptide potentially have a variety of functions, but any one important function is likely to be regulated by a number of different neuropeptides. Understanding of such subtle control is growing at a steady pace, but simple, easily described systems are unlikely to be found (26). A final factor to note is that though a particular peptide may play a variety of roles in adult health and disease, it may also have had other totally different roles during development from embryo to adult.

NEUROPEPTIDES AS BIOLOGICAL WARFARE AGENTS

The Canadian document on novel toxins and bioregulators was sent to all the state parties and observers at the Third Review Conference of the BTWC in 1991 with a cover note from the director of the Arms Control and Disarmament Division of External Affairs and International Trade in Ottawa (23). The fifty-six-page document is divided into five main chapters:

1. Introduction
2. Technological Changes and Peptide Toxins and Bioregulators
3. Novel Toxins and Bioregulators
4. Potential Dangers Due to Changes in Technology
5. Conclusions: Implications for the Biological and Toxin Weapons Convention

The third chapter, "Novel Toxins and Bioregulators," has thirteen subsections that deal with a series of different toxins and, particularly, peptide bioregulators:

3.1   Conotoxins
3.2   Sarafotoxin—endothelin
3.3   Bioregulators
3.4   Substance P
3.5   Thyroliberin (TRF)
3.6   Gonadoliberin (LRF)
3.7   Somatostatin (SS)
3.8   Neurotensin (NT)
3.9   Bombesin (BN)
3.10 Endorphins and enkephalins
3.11 Dynorphin
3.12 Oxytocin and vasopressins
3.13 Other peptides (23)

The diverse conotoxins of sea snails have been mentioned previously (see Chapter 3), whereas sarafotoxin/endothelin and Substance P have been dealt with in more detail here. The other peptides discussed in the Canadian document are well-known examples. It must be emphasized again, however, that each of these peptides is likely to serve diverse functions (Table 5.2) and that major body functions are likely to be under the control of multiple bioregulators (Table 5.3).

The body's control systems have evolved, as noted earlier, with high levels of redundancy and therefore stability. Nevertheless, these control systems may be disrupted by natural disease or deliberate attack. We will concentrate here on other sections of the Canadian document that deal with the question of why bioregulators are now of *military* importance. The introduction identifies its central concern over the increasing knowledge of peptides: "This paper examines the tremendous increase in our knowledge of recently identified peptides (toxins and bioregulators) that control biological activity. These advances have increased concern about the scope for misuse of toxins and bioregulators as weapons" (23). It then pinpoints the most important technological change: "Prior to 1975, the production of quantities of peptides that might be considered militarily significant was not possible. Scientific and commercial developments have now made it possible to produce such quantities of peptides" (23).

Three production methods—chemical synthesis, enzymatic synthesis, and recombinant DNA techniques—are identified. The paper notes that the dipeptide artificial sweetener aspartame (better known as NutraSweet) was produced cheaply, primarily by enzymatic synthesis, in quantities of 4 million kilograms per year in the late 1980s. Besides mentioning growing production capabilities, it then cited two other important aspects of the current situation. The first of these is again technical. The capabilities for artificial synthesis of these peptides by various means have facilitated manipulation of their structures in a variety of ways and allowed for the effects of the

Table 5.2 Some Effects of Peptides

Peptide	Site of Action	Function
Endogenous opioids	Spinal cord and brain stem	Induces analgesia; reduces pain; lowers blood pressure; depresses respiration
	Hypothalamus and limbic system	Decreases body temperature; increases feeding and drinking
	Ventral tegmental area; striatum	Induces euphoria; regulates locomotor activity
Vasopressin	Thalamus and limbic system	Regulates blood pressure; facilitates learning and memory
Substance P	Brain and spinal cord; hypothalamus	Transmits pain signals; increases arousal and activity
Neuropeptide Y	Hypothalamus and thalamus	Increases feeding and drinking; reduces blood pressure and body temperature; facilitates memory

Source: From reference 26.

Table 5.3 Some Regulatory Functions of Peptides

Function	Peptide Actions
Pain regulation	Substance P and bradykinin transmit pain signals. Opioids, cholecystokinin (CCK), and neurotensin inhibit pain signals.
Blood pressure	Angiotensin, corticotrophic releasing hormone (CRH), thyrotrophic hormone-releasing hormone (TRH), and bombesin increase blood pressure. Opioids and neuropeptide Y (NPY) decrease blood pressure.
Body temperature	Somatostatin and TRH elevate body temperature. Opioids, neurotensin, bombesin, NPY, and CCK lower body temperature.
Arousal level and motor activity	TRH, CRH, vasopressin, and Substance P increase arousal and locomotor activity. Delta sleep–inducing peptide, CCK, and neurotensin reduce arousal and motor activity.

Source: From reference 26.

modified chemicals to be tested. Second, less attention than warranted has been paid to the possible use of biological weapons as *incapacitants*. Given the new technical capabilities for manipulating and producing peptides, it is argued, their use as incapacitating agents cannot easily be discounted.

The second chapter gives more detail on the important technical changes. It notes, for example, that "[s]omatostatin is a 14-amino-acid hormone which regulates the release of growth hormone, glucogen, and insulin. It was among the first hormones made by genetic engineering and was the first for which a totally synthetic gene was used" (23). However, it is argued,

for peptides with thirty to thirty-five amino acids or fewer, the best economic method of production is by automated, solid-phase, *chemical* synthesis, that is, by a standard chemical method not involving living organisms or genetic engineering. A list of twenty-one peptide toxins and
bioregulators already synthesized by this method follows:

Angiotensin II
Bombesin (frog)
Bradykinin
Cholecystokinin
Dynorphin (1–13)
Alpha-endorphin
Beta-endorphin (ovine)
Gamma-endorphin
[Leu5]-enkaphalin
[Met5]-enkephalin
Gastrin I
Gastrin releasing peptide
Gonadoliberin
Neurotensin
Somatostatin
Substance P
Thyroliberin
Vasoactive intestinal peptide
Conotoxin G1
Endothelin
Sarafotoxin (23)

Because thousands of natural peptides or their analogues have been synthesized by this method, it has to be regarded as a mature technology used
regularly in many parts of the world.

The presence of both Substance P and endothelin in the previous
list will be noted, but the reference to the production of analogues is of particular importance because it links to one of the document's main conclusions. An analogue is defined in the glossary of the Canadian document as:

> A modified form of the original molecule of the toxin or bioregulator,
> made by chemical synthesis, genetic engineering, or by other means.
> Analogues of toxins and bioregulators fall into two classes: *agonists* that
> bind to the target receptor and cause a similar response to that of the orig-
> inal toxin or bioregulator; and *antagonists* that bind to the target recep-
> tor and may block the action of the original toxin or bioregulator. (em-
> phases added) (23)

Referring to biologically active peptides, it is argued that:

> Recently, in the field of structure-activity relationships, fragments or sub-stituted analogues have been found to be of equal or greater potency when compared to the parent molecule. They can also exhibit long-lasting or antagonistic activities. . . .
>
> This is in marked contrast to measuring the lethality of toxins. Extensive research to date on neurotoxins has shown that it is not possible to increase their potency. (23)

Thus, from this viewpoint, known bioregulators are more of a concern as future weapons because they can be easily manipulated to achieve very different or much enhanced effects on the victim.

The theme of the potential modification of peptide bioregulators is evident in the third chapter of the document where individual peptides are examined. In regard to the simple tripeptide thyroliberin, the document states: "Several hundred analogues of TRF have been synthesized. Some of the analogues are more potent than others, while some are selective in action on the central nervous system" (23). And in regard to gonadoliberin: "Potent and long-lasting analogues of LRF have been designed. . . . The [leutinizing hormone–]releasing potency of the most potent agonists . . . are about one hundred and fifty times LRF. Potent antagonists also have been designed" (23).

The changes in neurotensin activity could be even more dramatic, with modifications of the most important part of the sequence of amino acids yielding a substance 1,000 times more active than the natural compound. Also, it is possible to greatly enhance one aspect of a bioregulator's function while leaving another little affected. Hence, specific analogues of somatostatin "were one thousand seven hundred and fifty times as potent in inhibiting insulin than in inhibiting glucogen secretion" (23). It is well known that many analogues of enkephalin have been made in efforts to find a nonaddictive opiate, and these can be much more potent than the natural compounds (27).

Chapter 4 of the Canadian document begins with a summary of the three interrelated scientific and technical trends that, it suggests, have had such a significant impact on the development of novel agents:

1. Scientific advances, resulting in the development of several methods for the large-scale production of biologically active peptides;
2. Dramatic technical advances in the world-wide biotechnology industry, resulting in commercially validated processes involved in the production, purification, and delivery of peptides; and,
3. The beginnings of a scientific revolution in the understanding of the role of peptide bioregulators in controlling biological processes (23).

The careful differentiation between the known problem of extremely potent, lethal, peptide toxins and of unknown future modifications of bioregulatory peptides is again reinforced. In any given example, and probably because of evolutionary competition between attacker and victim, there has been strong selective pressure toward the *most potent* lethal toxin with which to target a particular cellular type in the victim. It is therefore argued that modification of toxins is unlikely to make them *more potent*. However, specific new means by which novel toxin agents might be developed, for example, through targeting new sites of action, are reviewed. Though modification is unlikely to increase toxin potency, for bioregulators, "this is not the case since these compounds are involved in *modulating* cellular activities. They do not have a single endpoint of functions as neurotoxins do" (emphasis added) (23).

It should be theoretically possible then to make more effective bioregulators. In practical terms, as the document records, it has been shown that it *is* possible to make modifications that significantly increase the activity of peptides. In military terms, the concomitant decrease in the dose required means that less material has to be produced and effectively dispersed in a weapon system. Furthermore, it is argued that the duration of action of a bioregulator may be extended by modifications that slow the rate of its degradation in the body. Finally, because bioregulators act at many different sites, the possibility arises of designing modifications of a peptide to achieve specific ends, for example, "of selectively affecting mental processes and many aspects of health, such as control of mood, consciousness, temperature control, sleep or emotions" (23). Though there is an obvious concentration on the potential development of a new class of incapacitating weapons, the possibility that small imbalances in these bioregulators could cause even death is clearly indicated.

The potential difficulties of dispersing peptide bioregulators are then set out. Botulinum toxin, a protein, is known to lose its activity quite rapidly when dispersed in the field. However, as will become apparent in Chapter 7, there may well be ways of protecting small peptide agents from environmental degradation, or of using robust nonpeptide mimics in place of vulnerable peptides.

Looking forward, it is anticipated that there will be continued improvements in productive capabilities, and it must be expected that highly specific analogues of naturally occurring bioregulators will become available. Particular stress is put on the possibility of these analogues being much more potent than the original natural regulator. All this may have a revolutionary impact: "The idea of incapacitating weapons is an old one. However, with the increased knowledge and use of bioregulators, the whole concept of incapacitating weapons will have to be reexamined" (23). It is even argued that reversible, militarily effective physical incapacitation may become possible.

The Canadian document was written by a contractor for the government and used open source literature to assess trends both then (1991) and for the immediate future. The U.S. government expressed similar concerns about bioregulators in documents for the 1991 Third Review Conference of the BTWC and again at the 1996 Fourth Review Conference (see Chapter 3). But has any real interest in bioregulators been demonstrated in modern offensive biological warfare programs? The answer, unfortunately, is yes.

THE SOVIET UNION

Following the agreement and entry into force of the Biological and Toxin Weapons Convention in the early 1970s, the Soviet Union undertook a massive expansion of its illegal offensive biological weapons program. The full dimensions of this program and the military objectives it was intended to serve have yet to be described and debated fully in the literature. However, a better understanding is becoming possible as more detailed accounts are published (28, 29, 30). These reveal, for example, that considerable effort was devoted to the development and production of the standard toxin agents, botulinum toxin and staphylococcal enterotoxin B.

Of direct relevance here is Ken Alibek's description of the development of novel weapons in Project Bonfire. As noted in Chapter 4, there was special interest in the results, presented to a meeting in 1989, of a particular experiment. The results concerned the genetic engineering of a toxin (that attacked the mammalian nervous system) into the bacterium *Yersinia pseudotuberculosis*. Rabbits had been made to breathe an aerosol containing this engineered organism. The rabbits displayed the usual symptoms of the bacterial infection, but in one test several rabbits also showed signs of another illness: "They twitched and lay still. Their hindquarters had been paralysed" (31).

According to Alibek, the room was absolutely silent as everyone realized the implications of the experiment. Scientists had infected the animal with the bacterium and caused an illness *and* enabled the bacterium to produce the toxin that affected the nervous system. In principle, therefore, it would be possible to get the bacterium to produce other toxins or even bioregulators: "A new class of weapons had been found. For the first time, we would be capable of producing weapons based on chemical substances produced naturally in the human body" (31).

Obviously, bioregulatory peptides were being discussed and not just toxins. The substances that might be engineered into a bacterium "could damage the nervous system, alter moods, trigger psychological changes, and even kill. Our heart is regulated by peptides. If present in unusually high doses, these peptides will lead to heart palpitations and, in rare cases, death" (31).

If this is the kind of work that existed a decade ago it seems unlikely that the threat from such new forms of biological weapon has disappeared or that it will not develop further in the future. Some such future developments are the subject of the next chapter.

REFERENCES

1. M. G. Hamilton (1998). Toxins: The emerging threat. *ASA Newsletter* 98, no. 3: 1, 20–26.

2. Russian Federation (1992). *Illustrative List of Potential BW Agents*. Ad Hoc Group of Governmental Experts to Identify and Examine Potential Verification Measures from a Scientific and Technical Standpoint. BWC/CONF.III/VEREX/WP.23, Geneva, 7 April.

3. This Week (1988). DNA and defence. *New Scientist* (17 December): 7.

4. United States (1996). *The Biological Chemical Warfare Threat: Biological Warfare: A Tutorial*. Washington, D.C.

5. FOA (1996). *FOA Briefing Book on Biological Weapons*. Umeå, Sweden: FOA.

6. SIPRI (1973). *CB Weapons Today*. Vol. 2 of *The Problem of Chemical and Biological Warfare*. Stockholm: Almqvist and Wiksell (for SIPRI).

7. J. D. Douglass, Jr. (1992). Who's holding the psychotoxins and DNA-altering compounds? *Armed Forces Journal International* (September): 50–52.

8. Letter Report (1990). *Incapacitating Agents, European Communist Countries: Low Molecular Weight Neurotoxins, Psychotropics, Alkaloids, Organofluorines, and Blue-Green Algal Toxins*. AST-1620R-100–90, U.S. Army Intelligence Agency, 16 July.

9. R. F. Highsmith (1998). *Endothelin: Molecular Biology, Physiology, and Pathology*. Totowa, N.J.: Humana Press.

10. C. R. Martin (1995). *Dictionary of Endocrinology and Related Biomedical Sciences*. Oxford: Oxford University Press.

11. C. H. V. Hoyle (1996). *Neuropeptides: Essential Data*. Chichester: John Wiley and Sons.

12. M. Yanagisawa et al. (1988). A novel potent vasoconstrictor peptide produced by vascular endothelial cells. *Nature* 332 (31 March): 411–415.

13. C. Takasaki et al. (1988). Sarafotoxins S6: Several isotoxins from *Atractaspis engaddensis* (burrowing asp) venom that affect the heart. *Toxicon* 26, no. 6: 543–548.

14. B. K. Kramer et al. (1997). Circulatory and myocardial effects of endothelin. *Journal of Molecular Medicine* 75, nos. 11–12: 886–890.

15. A. Inoue (1989). The human endothelin family: Three structurally and pharmacologically distinct isopeptides predicted by three separate genes. *Proceedings of the National Academy of Sciences* 86: 2863–2867.

16. T. Miyauchi and T. Masaki (1999). Pathophysiology of endothelin in the cardiovascular system. *Annual Review of Physiology* 61: 391–415.

17. A. Benigni and G. Remuzzi (1999). Endothelin antagonists. *The Lancet* 353: 133–138.

18. D. J. Webb et al. (1998). Endothelin: New discoveries and rapid progress in the clinic. *TiPS* 19 (January): 5–8.

19. B. L. Koch et al. (1999). Inhalation of Substance P and thiorphan: Acute toxicity and effects on respiration in conscious guinea pigs. *Journal of Applied Toxicology* 19: 19–23.

20. J. E. Maggio and P. W. Mantyh (1994). History of tachykinin peptides. In S. H. Buck, ed., *The Tachykinin Receptors*. Totowa, N.J.: Humana Press, pp. 1–22.

21. Y. Q. Cao et al. (1998). Primary afferent tachykinins are required to experience moderate to intense pain. *Nature* 392 (26 March): 390–394.

22. C. De Felipe et al. (1998). Altered nociception, analgesia and aggression in mice lacking the receptor for Substance P. *Nature* 392 (26 March): 394–397.

23. Canada (1991). *Novel Toxins and Bioregulators: The Emerging Scientific and Technological Issues Relating to Verification and the Biological and Toxin Weapons Convention*. External Affairs and International Trade, Ottawa, Canada, September.

24. N. H. Sector (1990). Neuroimmunomodulation takes off. *Immunology Today* 11, no. 11: 381–383.

25. S. A. Binkley (1995). *Endocrinology*. London: HarperCollins.

26. R. E. Brown (1994). *An Introduction to Neuroendocrinology*. Cambridge: Cambridge University Press.

27. M. R. Dando (1996). *A New Form of Warfare: The Rise of Non-Lethal Weapons*. London: Brassey's.

28. M. Leitenberg (1996). Biological weapons arms control. *Contemporary Security Policy* 17, no. 1: 1–79.

29. G. Bozheyeva et al. (1999). *Former Soviet Biological Weapons Facilities in Kazakhstan: Past, Present, Future*. Occasional Paper No. 1. Center for Non-Proliferation Studies, Monterey Institute of International Studies.

30. D. Litovkin (1999). Valentin Yevstigneyev on issues relating to Russian biological weapons. *Yaderny Kontrol* (Digest) 11: 43–51.

31. K. Alibek and S. Handelman (1999). *Biohazard*. New York: Random House.

6

Specificity: Receptors

Any reasoned analysis of the present international system must conclude that the early decades of the twenty-first century will be marked by considerable instability and conflict (1, 2). The gap between the minority rich and majority poor of the world is already immense and likely to widen, and population growth in poorer, resource-deficient regions will not come under control for some time yet.

In addition to these underlying drivers of instability, one net result of the long East-West Cold War in the second half of the twentieth century was to flood conflict-prone regions of the developing world with the weaponry that will continue to exacerbate the conflicts that arise there. To make the situation potentially even more unstable, another consequence of the vast expenditure of resources on weapons development by the rich world over the past fifty years has been to produce what is called a "revolution in military affairs" (RMA) (3). We do not need to discuss the details of this revolution here, but we should note that its key characteristics include the application of modern information technology to weapon systems and their use. In one sense, as seen in the wars in the Gulf in 1991 and the former Yugoslavia in 1999, this leads to the capability for much more discriminating use of force (4). However, it has to be accepted that advanced weapon systems such as cluster bombs can have immense destructive power, and the capability to target numerous discriminating weapons at the same place at the same time can lead to enormous devastation. So the development of the RMA does not necessarily imply that wars can be fought with few casualties and little damage. Indeed, it could well be that the very opposite is the case in certain circumstances.

Whatever the developments in technology, though, it has been acknowledged since the nineteenth century that any state's right to wage war is not unlimited. The most recent statement of this principle was made in

87

the 1977 Protocol 1 Additional to the Geneva Conventions of 1949. In Part III of this protocol, which applies to "Methods and Means of Warfare Combatant and Prisoner-of-War Status," Article XXXV on basic rules states, in part:

1. In any armed conflict, the right of the Parties to the conflict to choose methods or means of warfare is not unlimited.
2. It is prohibited to employ weapons, projectiles and materials and methods of warfare of a nature *to cause superfluous injury or unnecessary suffering.* (emphasis added) (5)

Moreover, in relation to new forms of weaponry, Article XXXVI on new weapons states: "In the study, development, acquisition of a new weapon, means or method of warfare, a High Contracting Party is under an obligation to determine whether its employment would, in some or all circumstances, be prohibited by this Protocol or by any other rule of international law applicable to the High Contracting Party" (5). These restrictions on methods and means of warfare apply to the use of weapons against combatants as well as noncombatants. Unfortunately, it has historically been difficult to reach agreement on how to define "superfluous injury or unnecessary suffering."

At the end of the twentieth century, a century in which a conflict-prone world had been awash with weapons, and in which new weapons with revolutionary characteristics were being developed and deployed, it was hardly surprising that the International Committee of the Red Cross had been considering whether it could do anything more to help limit the resulting devastation. In 1996 it organized a symposium on the medical profession and the effects of weapons, and since that time has been developing the SIrUS (Superfluous Injury or Unnecessary Suffering) project to assist policymakers in making judgments on the legality of weapons under international humanitarian law (6).

The SIrUS project collected data on the effects of weapons used in recent conflicts—particularly from the ICRC's own wounds database. It looked at a wide range of these effects and determined that weapons causing injury by explosions or projectiles only and that do not target a specific part of the body as a function of their design typically:

• Do not cause a field mortality of more than 22 percent nor a hospital mortality of more than 5 percent;
• Cause grade 3 wounds (a Red Cross wound-classification measurement) in less than 10 percent of survivors sent to the hospital;
• Can be treated for the most part by well-established medical and surgical methods (7).

The experts involved in the project were trying to discover criteria by which an objective distinction could be made between such weapons and the effects of all other weapons. The criteria proposed by the SIrUS project, in order to make such a distinction, clearly related to *the foreseeable and design-dependent effects of weapons when used against humans:* The criteria suggested on what constitutes superfluous injury and unnecessary suffering follow:

- Specific disease, specific abnormal physiological state, specific abnormal psychological state, specific and permanent disability, or specific disfigurement (Criterion 1); or
- Field mortality of more than 25 percent or hospital mortality of more than 5 percent (Criterion 2); or
- Grade 3 wounds as measured by the Red Cross wound classification (Criterion 3); or
- Effects for which there is no well-recognized and proven treatment (Criterion 4) (5).

Though a rifle bullet or fragmentation weapon *may* cause severe wounds (grade 3 wounds) or death, this will depend on where the person is hit or where he or she is in relation to the explosion. The crucial point is that some weapons can be expected to inflict certain effects on virtually *every* occasion, and these consequences result from the nature of the technology of the weapon, that is, they are design dependent. If, for example, someone steps on an antipersonnel mine, that person will almost certainly receive a severe (grade 3) injury. Similarly, a blinding laser will inflict specific and permanent disability, if the eyes are hit, for which there is no proven medical treatment. And, clearly, biological weapons inflict specific disease or an abnormal physiological state whenever a person is infected.

The ICRC continues to work toward getting these criteria widely accepted and implemented by states. At the same time, the developing revolution in biology and medicine is providing more and more ways in which specific body systems may be targeted. It is important from our perspective to acknowledge and appreciate the underlying reasons why this will happen and therefore why the development of international law is so essential at this time.

CELL SIGNALING

Why are members of the medical profession so concerned that a specific attack on body functions is becoming much more of a potential threat? To answer this question, it is necessary to look in greater detail at modern research on how organisms are coordinated.

All organisms, or the cells within an organism, must have the ability to sense the significant chemicals in their particular environments and respond appropriately. Without that ability, they could not survive for long. How else could an organism avoid certain kinds of danger, or the cells within an organism develop into different kinds of tissues and organ systems? Scientists have known for many years that the necessary cellular communication through chemical signals is quite complex. In the nineteenth century, as discussed in Chapter 2, Charles Darwin suggested that there must be a chemical signaling system in plants. Modern research techniques have made possible the discovery that signaling systems are surprisingly similar across the whole range of living organisms, plants and animals, and have facilitated the further discovery of how extremely specific they are (8).

A short consideration of the kinds of chemicals that would make for good signals between cells will quickly lead to the conclusion that they should preferably have small molecules (and thus be able to move easily) and that it would be advantageous if they could be made and degraded quickly. In that way they could be produced when required, exert their precise effect, and then be quickly switched off so that their effect did not persist beyond the required period. As indicated in previous chapters, such signaling chemicals are found as neurotransmitters in the nervous system and as hormones in the endocrine system.

One common method of studying such chemical signaling systems is to try to discover how a chemical's effects are enhanced or inhibited by systematically changing its structure and testing the effects of the new, slightly different chemical. Another method has been to use molecular biology (genetic engineering) to disrupt a particular part of a cell's signaling system and to find out what consequences follow from the disruption. The interaction between enhanced information technology and the growing capabilities of molecular biologists has been important in generating new discoveries. Because there are considerable similarities in the signaling systems in different organisms, there is a great advantage in being able to search the many genome and protein sequence databases. Computer analysis has also become increasingly useful in modeling the structural changes that might come about in a protein if changes are made in amino acid sequences and for following the complex network of changes that can occur in a cell after a signal is received. Our main concern here is with the way in which external chemical signals are recognized by the cell. This in itself is a vast area of research, and we shall briefly review some of the key elements of direct interest in regard to bioregulatory peptides and toxins.

In a multicellular organism like a human being, cells can communicate by direct transfer of small chemical molecules (across what are called gap junctions) or through the detection of outer membrane proteins if the cells should come into close contact. However, one of the most important ways in which cells communicate is through the release of small signaling molecules that are released by one cell and detected by others, as in the nervous and endocrine systems. In the endocrine system such chemicals—hormones—can be released at a great distance from the targeted cell. The concentration of a hormone in the blood system will inevitably be quite low because of all the other constituents that are present in blood. What is it then that gives specificity to the interaction between the signaling chemicals and the target cells they affect?

RECEPTORS

The concentration of a signal chemical is most likely to be low, so the target cell needs to have very sensitive receptors (usually on the outer membrane of the cell) that will bind to a signaling chemical with very high affinity. Only then can the signal chemical have a high probability of exerting its effect. The standard terminology names the signaling chemical the *ligand,* and the binding of the ligand to the *cell receptor* is the stimulus for the consequential events that occur within the cell.

Despite the huge range of extracellular molecules encountered by the individual cells of organisms, and the vast array of different types of cell within organisms, it has been possible to classify receptors into a small number of similar types. Two of these are of particular interest here.

G Protein–Coupled Receptors

When this class of receptor is activated by the binding of its ligand, there is activation of a G protein that conveys the message to the next component of the intracellular signal pathway. The structure of these receptors is well known (9). Each consists of a chain of amino acids that passes to and fro across the cell membrane seven times. So there is an initial part of the chain *outside* the cell, then the seven transitions into and out of the cell, and finally a terminal segment of the chain *inside* the cell. The seven crossings of the cell membrane made by the chain of amino acids are not in a straight line but, rather, form a circle, in the middle of which is the central core of the receptor. Many well-known neurotransmitters and neuropeptides function by binding to such receptors.

Ligand-Gated Ion Channel Receptors

Because ions carry an electrical charge, they cannot pass through the charged cell membrane in the absence of special ion channels. These channels cannot be permanently open, otherwise ions would continually flood in or out, so mechanisms have to be provided for opening and closing the channels. One such mechanism is provided by ligand-gated ion channel receptors. Here the binding of the ligand to the receptor changes the permeability of the cell membrane to the ion because the receptor undergoes a change of structure that effectively opens the channel. However, these receptor systems are involved in more rapid changes than those of the G protein–linked receptors, and the receptor quickly returns to its former state. The structures of these ligand-gated ion channel receptors are more diverse than those of the G protein–linked receptors. The receptors are made up of groups of proteins that cluster around the ion channel in the membrane. This fast type of cell receptor is of particular interest because its function can be disrupted in various ways by diverse toxins. The best-known neurotransmitter, acetylcholine, acts as a ligand for both G protein–linked and ligand-gated ion channel receptors (the so-called muscarinic and nicotinic receptors, respectively). Botulinum toxin, which acts to prevent release of acetylcholine from the presynaptic nerve terminals, thus affects both muscarinic and nicotinic systems.

The Pace of Change

The structure of a particular receptor is appropriate for the binding of a particular ligand. This is what gives unique specificity to the interaction and thus to the signaling channel. Receptors are proteins made up of long chains of different amino acids. The twenty amino acids found commonly in the human body have different structures; thus, changes in the sequence of amino acids in a receptor will change the overall structure of the receptor because the protein will take on a different final shape (10). The more we learn about cell receptors, the more we can potentially interfere with their operation for both benign purposes (when they malfunction in disease) or for malign purposes to construct new biological weapons.

What is quite remarkable is the rate at which knowledge of receptors and their ligands has accumulated over the past decade. A report in 1999, *TiPS Receptor and Ion Channel Nomenclature,* was introduced by its editors in this way: "Looking back, it is apparent that the past decade has brought an enormous increase in knowledge about the pharmacology and structural biology of receptors and ion channels" (11). The first edition, in 1990, contained thirty pages of listings, only 25 percent of which had primary sequence information (on the structure of the receptor). In contrast, in 1999 the editors wrote: "In this tenth edition, 106 pages are required to accommodate current information on approximately 50 receptor and ion channel classes, for which structural information is presented for over 99%" (11).

Many of the classes of receptors and ion channels have been shown to have numerous subtypes. So, although the listing includes ion channels that are not ligand-gated (that is, receptors that work by different mechanisms to those discussed here), the actual number of known receptors is much higher than the fifty *classes* listed. The growth in knowledge in this area of research over the past decade is truly remarkable and reflects both enabling scientific and technical breakthroughs *and* the high levels of investment in pursuit of new medical drugs.

Against that background it is pertinent to ask what we know of the receptors for endothelin and Substance P.

Endothelin. Endothelin was discovered in the late 1980s. The authors of a major review of the subject in 1994 stated that they were unable to cover all the 2,500 original research papers that had been written since endothelin's discovery, but they pointed out that "[s]ix years later, it is now evident that the discovery of the ET peptide [endothelin] family initiated a new field of biomedical research which promises to lead to better understanding of the pathomechanisms of several diseases and to the development of novel therapeutics" (12).

By the mid-1990s, for example, three different ET genes had been identified at different locations on the human genome, and these genes, which were differentially regulated, led to the expression of three different endothelins: ET-1, ET-2, and ET-3. As discussed briefly in Chapter 5, there are two endothelin receptors, ET_A and ET_B (11). Both are of the G protein–linked class. The rank order of affinity of the endothelins for the ET_A receptor is ET-1 greater or equal to ET-2 and then ET-3, whereas for the ET_B receptor, the endothelins have about equal affinity.

At one level, the effects of these peptides are simple and straightforward: "Endothelin is a potent vasoconstrictor. . . . Its cardiovascular actions are mediated by endothelin-A and endothelin-B receptors" (13). These receptors, however, have opposing functions: "In the vasculature, stimulation of endothelin-A receptors on vascular smooth-muscle cells causes vasoconstriction, whereas stimulation of endothelin-B receptors on endothelial cells generally causes vasodilation. In man, vasoconstrictor effects predominate" (13). This, of course, was the basis of the surmised endothelin use in the terrorist attack scenario described in Chapter 5. Such cardiovascular influence, though, is far from the end of the story. Endothelin acts as a local hormone in vascular smooth muscle in humans, but it is also known to exert other effects (14). Endothelin seems to be involved in the series of malfunctions that occur in heart failure. Heart failure is a primary cause of death in the developed world, so it is hardly surprising that so much work continues on the endothelin system. It has also been shown that mice rendered incapable—through genetic engineering—of producing ET-1 die at birth from respiratory failure and exhibit major deformities; this suggests that ET-1 is essential for normal development (15).

Notwithstanding the complexity of its effects, it does appear that the level of ET-1 production is raised in the process of chronic heart failure (CHF). The raised level of ET-1 is helpful in the short term, assisting the heart to recover after heart failure, but it also has longer-term damaging effects on the heart muscle. The raised level acts through the endothelin receptors, and a major possible route to alleviating further heart failure might therefore be to find antagonists that block the receptors and prevent the elevated ET-1 levels from exerting their damaging effects. As one recent experimental report on rats argued: "[T]he upregulated myocardial endothelin system aggravated the progression of CHF, [but] . . . long-term (12 weeks) treatment with the endothelin antagonist BQ123 greatly improved the survival rate of rats with CHF as a result of myocardial infarction" (16).

The antagonist blocked the action of endothelin and reduced longer-term cardiac damage. It is obvious that any drug company that develops an effective long-term endothelin antagonist will very likely earn large sums of money over a protracted period. The race to develop such chemicals is well under way and guarantees that we shall soon have a much greater knowledge of the endothelin system and of how its receptors function. That will be invaluable in dealing with a major medical problem, but, given the dual-use nature of the knowledge, it could also allow for much more sophisticated means of misusing endothelin-like substances to attack human beings. How such substances are developed will be investigated after a review of recent work on Substance P.

Substance P.   The standard listing of receptors referred to earlier includes three tachykinin receptors NK_1, NK_2, and NK_3 (11). The ligands for these receptors are Substance P, neurokinin A (previously known by other names, including neurokinin α) and neurokinin B (previously known by other names, including neurokinin β). The order of affinity of these ligands for NK_1 receptors is Substance P, neurokinin A, and then neurokinin B; for NK_2 it is neurokinin A, neurokinin B, and then Substance P; and finally for NK_3 it is neurokinin B, neurokinin A, and then Substance P.

Though the endothelins are located and act in *peripheral* endothelial cells, tachykinins such as Substance P and neurokinin A probably play their most important physiological roles as part of the central nervous system. The role of (neuro)peptides in the CNS is significant, but its discovery is quite recent. Until the 1960s, it was generally accepted that the nervous system had only a small number, probably less than ten, of neurotransmitter substances that passed information between neurons and between neurons and effector systems like muscles: "Today, the situation is entirely different, and it is generally believed that the number of neuro-transmitters is much larger, probably [greater than] 50" (17). Moreover: "The main reason for this change is the recent introduction of a large number [greater than] 20 of putative peptide neurotransmitters. Among these putative peptide neurotransmitters SP [Substance P] and a few others . . . are those whose transmitter roles are somewhat firmly established" (17).

As reviewed in Chapter 5, Substance P is considered to be the neuro-transmitter for a particular type of pain-sensitive sensory neuron widely distributed in the body. Moreover, damage to peripheral tissues not only causes these sensory neurons to send (pain) information into the CNS but also provokes them into releasing Substance P at their peripheral terminals. This contributes to the inflammatory response to the original damage.

It is now thought that neurokinin receptors play significant roles in a very diverse set of diseases:

> The ability of SP and NKA [neurokinin A] to provoke a number of responses in the airway, including bronchoconstriction, vasodilation, inflammatory cell infiltration, mucus secretion . . . has led to suggestions that these mediators and their cognate [related] receptors may be involved in the initiation or exacerbation of asthma and other inflammatory airway disorders. (18)

There is also considerable evidence for the role of NK_1 receptors in the initiation of vomiting, for example, in response to motion and also in migraine headaches (18, 19).

It seems that Substance P and neurokinin A are encoded by a single gene called PPT-A, which gives rise to a number of ribonucleic acids through splicing (splitting up of the original RNA into smaller pieces, which then determine the structure of different peptides or proteins). The gene for neurokinin B, PPT-B, is similar in structure to PPT-A but is expressed to different extents in different tissues: "In human asthma, mRNA [messenger RNA] expression of NK_1 and NK_2 receptors increases. Exposure of animals to allergen enhances levels of PPT-A in the nodose ganglion (the major sensory supply to the airways) concomitant with a 3–4 fold rise in SP and NKA in the lung" (20).

Though infrequently as immediately dangerous as CHF, all these human health problems—asthma, motion sickness, and migraines—are of considerable concern to society, and so there are good reasons for medical research to be carried out on the implicated receptor systems. However, it will be recalled that the defense scientists studying the effects of Substance P had to add an extra chemical to their aerosol in order to prevent the body's normal enzymes from quickly destroying the peptide. This rapid destruction is likely to happen to any peptide, and therefore the search for more potent ligands or antagonists is not simple. Researchers are nevertheless making enormous and rapid strides in such developments, particularly with regard to nonpeptide chemicals that mimic the effects of agonists or function as antagonists. The question is, How did the quest for new therapeutic chemicals become so efficient? If that question can be answered, it will be much easier to see how the threat from bioregulators (and perhaps also toxins) might evolve in the next few decades.

Drug Development

For centuries, societies have produced herbals of diverse plants for treating various ailments, and modern research has shown that there are indeed appropriately active substances in many of the plants used. However, the scientific development of effective drugs did not begin until the early nineteenth century. As knowledge of chemistry developed, it proved possible, for example, for Friedrich Setürner to purify morphine from crude opium in 1806; and by the end of the century, Paul Ehrlich was able to demonstrate that pathogenic infections could be treated by administering specific chemicals (21). As we saw in Chapter 2, the standard approach developed by the 1930s was for a "lead compound" to be subjected to systematic modification so that the most active—and least toxic—of its derivatives could be discovered. Knowledge of the body's functional systems remained very limited, though, and in spite of much effort going into "rational design" of drugs, analysis shows that there are few examples of rational design of "wonder drugs" from the twentieth century. A much more frequent origin has been a serendipitous discovery—often, of course, by an observant scientist capable of spotting a significant new phenomenon. Alexander Fleming's discovery of penicillin is a famous example.

Following World War II, a highly sophisticated quantitative approach to drug design became possible, but in the absence of knowledge about the structure of the biological receptor on which the variously modified substances were acting. This all changed with the advent of modern molecular biology: "Cloning of genes, the discovery and use of polymeric chain reaction (PCR) to produce large quantities of the gene in a short time, and the expression of the gene to produce the desired biomolecule in needed quantities have made it possible to actually carry out specific receptor-ligand interactions in the laboratory" (21). With this level of knowledge, it became possible to start deciphering the three-dimensional structure of the receptor and how the ligand interacts with this structure. Furthermore, the revolution in information technology has provided new tools for carrying out such work: "[T]he computer technology evolving at a rapid pace has made available a number of software packages that allow a visual on-screen study of the receptor-ligand binding in order to arrive at structures with optimum levels of desired activity" (21). So we are now in the era of computer-aided molecular design and computer-aided drug design.

The implications for offensive biological warfare programs of this kind of capability were stated by Murrray Hamilton in his article "Toxins: The Emerging Threat": "It is apparent that a significant program of new threat (toxin or mid-spectrum) agent development could be undertaken with a very modest outlay of resources" (22). He suggests that such "virtual" development of a new agent could be done almost anywhere by a small team and that validation (testing) of the results would only be required in the final stages. Furthermore, when such final testing was required, advances in the production of large numbers of related compounds by combinatorial chemistry and the robotic testing of such drugs by high-throughput screening techniques would mean that extremely powerful new technologies could be applied (23, 24). It is little wonder then that rapid advances are now being made in drug design—and possibly also in agent design.

The impact of these advancing scientific and technological capabilities can be seen in relation to efforts to develop usable antagonists to ET-1 at ET_A receptors. Though the earliest reports were of peptide compounds being developed, the great advantages of *nonpeptide* antagonists, and the probable utility of such compounds in treating heart disease, has led to the development of many new compounds, some of which are going into clinical testing (25, 26). What is obvious, even from a limited analysis of a small selection of the research papers published on this subject, is the rational/mechanistic analysis that has now become possible in designing the work, strongly supporting the view that much further rapid progress will be possible (27, 28, 29, 30, 31). It is not surprising that a mid-1990s major review, "Receptors and Antagonists for Substance P and Related Peptides," concluded: "Application of molecular modeling to peptides and especially to new small peptide or nonpeptide antagonists, combined with receptor mutagenesis, should contribute to an understanding of the architecture of the active receptor site and lead to rational design of antagonists" (32).

It also argued that that goal would likely be achieved quite soon for the NK_1 receptor. The situation in regard to neuropeptides and G protein–linked receptors is more complex and much more interesting than even this spectacular account might suggest.

The effect of the genomics revolution has been to vastly increase the number of putative G protein–linked receptors known. They are called "orphan" receptors because their natural ligands are as yet unknown. One article on such orphan receptors summarized that by traditional molecular genetic approaches, coupled with the explosion in genomics information, more than 100 additional orphan G protein–coupled receptor family members have been identified (33).

There is enough sequence information to identify these receptors as belonging to the G protein–linked group but often insufficient sequence correspondence with known receptors to assign their ligands or predict their function. The authors stated that at the time of the review there were more than 240 human receptors of this type, and as the information in databases grew, their number was expected to increase considerably.

The impact of genomics over the past decade has, in fact, overturned the traditional approach to drug discovery. It is worth remembering that even endothelin was discovered using the traditional approach—where research began with the discovery of a functional activity and isolation of a ligand. Characterization of this ligand then led to discovery of its receptor. This method has now radically changed, with research starting from bioinformatics and molecular genetics in what is called "reverse molecular pharmacology" (Table 6.1). This approach determines the structure of the receptor first and only then leads on to the ligand. With the known linkage of other G protein–linked receptors to important disease states, and a track record of useful drug discovery in relation to such receptors, this approach is bound to be intensively pursued by drug companies (34).

We have been dealing here with the impact of genomics on just one aspect of the work of the pharmaceutical industry, and it is important to grasp, as Antoon J. M. Van Oosterhoat recently wrote, that "[t]he rapid advance of this field and its impact on the [entire] pharmaceutical industry cannot be overstated" (35). In his view, the most important areas of work include the joining of classical genetics and biology of model organisms to genomic information. It has long been known that, due to differences in genetic makeup, some individuals metabolize drugs in different ways (36). Some of these ways can lead to serious health complications, and thus "pharmacogenetics" is important for the industry. What, however, is the significance of model organisms, on which tests of probable relevance for humans can be carried out?

As genomic information has accumulated for different organisms, it has become possible to draw conclusions about the relationship between genes in different species (37). In particular: "Orthologs are genes in different species that evolved from a common ancestral gene by speciation [formation of new species types]; by contrast paralogs are genes related by duplication within a genome" (38). Normally, orthologs retain the same function during evolution whereas paralogs tend to develop new functions.

Table 6.1   Chronology of Different Approaches to Drug Discovery

Classical	Reverse Molecular Pharmacology
1. Functional activity	1. Bioinformatics/molecular genetics
2. Ligand	2. Receptor
3. Biological role/pathophysiology	3. Ligand
4. Receptor	4. Compound screening
5. Compound screening	5. Biological role/pathophysiology
6. Clinical development	6. Clinical development

Source: From reference 33.

The relationship between human genes and the genes of related animals is partly why the implications of the genomics revolution in biology and medicine far exceed the simple capability to clone a gene (39). In 1990 the gene for the ligand endothelin was cloned (40). By 1999 it was possible to show how blockage of the endothelin type A (ET_A) receptor prevented the atherosclerosis that could lead to myocardial infarction in a *susceptible strain of mice,* and for this to be seen as a significant advance in our understanding of the mechanism leading to heart attack in *humans* (41).

Without an understanding of the underlying rate of development in genomics and related science and technology, the kinds of *defensive research* projects being carried out—for example, by the U.S. Defense Advanced Research Projects Agency to combat the possible use of biological weapons—can have an almost science fiction aspect to them (42). How else can projects such as counting different DNA bases by passing the single-stranded material through a bacterial ion channel at a rate of about one base per millisecond be explained? The aim of such work, essentially, is to acquire the ability to detect different types of pathogens extremely rapidly and thus the ability to take effective action against an attack. A U.S. Air Force study concluded that by the year 2020:

> The critical aspects of warfighting in the C/B environment will be solved. Agent detection, both on-site and standoff will be available. In the event of an attack, equipment and critical terrain can be rapidly decontaminated. . . . Our ability to model this environment, coupled with our known ability to fight successfully under these conditions, will be a major deterrent to the use of C/B weapons. (43)

That is the hopeful scenario; but it is also possible that an arms race of considerable proportions could result as *offensive* research is attempted in order to overcome the strengthened defense. We know, after all, that misperceptions of other countries' intentions have in the past provoked the initiation of offensive biological weapons programs in major states, and it can be expected that this process would accelerate should major countries become involved in warfare in which there is even a threat of biological weapons use (44, 45). Moreover, the overwhelming military capabilities of the developed world are not certain to guarantee protection. Military analysts who have examined current U.S. predominance point out that it is not necessary for a rival to try to emulate such capabilities. Another possible response is the offset, a set of countermeasures to disrupt superior military capabilities. A further response is to bypass the superior country by "developing new means of warfare to leapfrog the rival's capabilities, or methods of operation designed to avoid dealing with them" (46).

So, if the United States has massive conventional superiority well into the twenty-first century and also develops means of protecting its forces against biological attack, that does not necessarily forestall attack on the United States by bioterrorists, or biological attack on allies that hinders U.S. military intervention in an unstable region.

In that regard, it is important to note that the genomics revolution does not just involve studies of the human genome and those of closely related species. For example, recently there have been tremendous advances in our understanding of the genomes of important staple crops and of the genomes of viruses that attack vital stock animals (47, 48). These advances are significant because recent estimates suggest that, of the 30,000 scientists and technicians involved in the offensive biological weapons program of the former Soviet Union in the 1980s, some one-third—that is, 10,000 qualified people—worked on agriculture-related issues (49).

The targeted attacks that are a future possibility will be further addressed later, after a consideration, in Chapter 7, of how an agent could be delivered to its target.

REFERENCES

1. P. Rogers and M. R. Dando (1992). *A Violent Peace: Global Security After the Cold War.* London: Brassey's.

2. P. M. Hughes (1999). A prepared statement at a hearing on Global Threats and Challenges: The Decades Ahead. Senate Armed Services Committee. Washington, D.C., 2 February.

3. S. Metz (1998). "NLW and the revolution in military affairs (RMA)." Paper presented to the conference NLW '98: Non-Lethal Weapons: Developments and Doctrine. Jane's Information Group, London, 1–2 December.

4. A. Truesdell (1997). *Discriminate Warfare: Evolving Military Technologies and Practices.* Bailrigg Memorandum 24. Centre for Defence and International Security Studies, Lancaster University.

5. R. M. Coupland, ed. (1997). Appendix 2 of *The SIrUS Project.* International Committee of the Red Cross.

6. International Committee of the Red Cross (1996). *The Medical Profession and the Effects of Weapons.* Report of the Symposium, Montreux, Switzerland, 8–10 March.

7. P. Herby (1999). "Meeting of experts on the SIrUS project." Paper presented at the International Committee of the Red Cross, Geneva, 10–11 May.

8. J. T. Hancock (1997). *Cell Signalling.* Edinburgh: Longman.

9. S. M. Stahl (1996). *Essential Psychopharmacology: Neuroscientific Basis and Clinical Applications.* Cambridge: Cambridge University Press.

10. G. L. Patrick (1995). *An Introduction to Medicinal Chemistry.* Oxford: Oxford University Press.

11. S. Alexander et al. (1999). *TiPS Receptor and Ion Channel Nomenclature Supplement 1999.* Cambridge: Elsevier Trends Journals.

12. G. M. Rubanyi and M. A. Polokoff (1994). Endothelins: Molecular biology, biochemistry, pharmacology, physiology and pathophysiology. *Pharmacological Reviews* 46, no. 3: 325–415.

13. M. M. Givertz and W. S. Colucci (1998). New targets for heart-failure therapy: Endothelin, inflammatory cytokines and oxidative stress. *The Lancet* (Supplement) 352: 34–38.

14. A. Benigzani and G. Remuzzi (1999). Endothelin antagonists. *The Lancet* 353: 133–138.

15. Y. Kurihan et al. (1994). Elevated blood pressure and craniofascial abnormalities in mice deficient in endothelin-1. *Nature* 368 (21 April): 703–710.

16. T. Miyauchi and K. Goto (1999). Heart failure and endothelin receptor antagonists. *TiPS* 20 (May): 211–217.

17. M. Otsuka and Y. Koichi (1993). Neurotransmitter functions of mammalian tachykinins. *Physiological Reviews* 73, no. 2: 229–308.

18. S. G. Mills (1997). Recent advances in neurokinin receptor antagonists. *Annual Reports in Medicinal Chemistry* 32: 51–60.

19. C. J. Swain and R. J. Hargreaves (1996). Neurokinin receptor antagonists. *Annual Reports in Medicinal Chemistry* 31: 111–120.

20. C. J. Ohnmacht, Jr. (1998). Recent advances in neurokinin receptor antagonists. *Annual Reports in Medicinal Chemistry* 33: 71–80.

21. P. N. Kaul (1998). Drug discovery: Past, present and future. *Progress in Drug Research* 50: 9–106.

22. M. G. Hamilton (1998). Toxins: The emerging threat. *ASA Newsletter* 93, no. 3: 1, 20–28.

23. M. J. Plunkett and J. A. Ellman (1997). Combinatorial chemistry and new drugs. *Scientific American*, April, pp. 54–59.

24. B. A. Kenny et al. (1998). The application of high-throughput screening to novel lead discovery. *Progress in Drug Research* 51: 245–270.

25. M. A. Lago et al. (1996). Endothelin antagonists. *Annual Reports in Medicinal Chemistry* 31: 81–90.

26. S. A. Douglas (1997). Clinical development of endothelin receptor antagonists. *TiPS* 18 (November): 408–412.

27. H. Riechers et al. (1996). Discovery and optimization of a novel class of orally active nonpeptidic endothelin-A receptor antagonists. *Journal of Medicinal Chemistry* 39: 2123–2128.

28. T. F. Walsh (1995). Progress in the development of endothelin receptor antagonists. *Annual Reports in Medicinal Chemistry* 30: 91–100.

29. J. J. Maguire et al. (1997). Affinity and selectivity of PD156707, a novel nonpeptide endothelin antagonist, for human ET_A and ET_B receptors. *Journal of Pharmacology and Experimental Therapeutics* 280, no. 2: 1102–1108.

30. T. Hoshino et al. (1998). Pharmacological profile of T-0201, a highly potent and orally active endothelin receptor antagonist. *Journal of Pharmacology and Experimental Therapeutics* 286, no. 2: 643–649.

31. E. H. Ohlstein et al. (1998). Nonpeptide endothelin receptor antagonists. No. 11. Pharmacological characterization of SB 234551, a high-affinity and selective nonpeptide ET_A receptor antagonist. *Journal of Pharmacology and Experimental Therapeutics* 286, no. 2: 650–656.

32. D. Regoli et al. (1994). Receptors and antagonists for Substance P and related peptides. *Pharmacological Reviews* 46, no. 4: 551–599.

33. J. M. Stadel et al. (1997). Orphan G protein–coupled receptors: A neglected opportunity for pioneer drug discovery. *TiPS* 18 (November): 430–437.

34. C. Betancur et al. (1997) Nonpeptide antagonists of neuropeptide receptors: Tools for research and therapy. *TiPS* 18 (October): 372–386.

35. A. J. M. Van Oosterhout (1998). Genomics and drug discovery. *TiPS* 19 (May): 157–160.

36. W. Kalow (1997). Pharmacogenetics in biological perspective. *Pharmacological Reviews* 49, no. 4: 369–379.

37. S. Henikoff et al. (1997). Gene families: The taxonomy of protein paralogs and chimeras. *Science* 278 (24 October): 609–614.

38. R. L. Tatusov (1997). A genomic perspective on protein families. *Science* 278 (24 October): 631–637.

39. T. A. Brown (1999). *Genomes.* Oxford: BIOS Scientific Publishers.

40. H. Arai et al. (1990). Cloning and expression of a cDNA encoding an endothelin receptor. *Nature* 348 (20, 27 December): 730–732.

41. G. Galiguiri et al. (1999). Myocardial infarction mediated by endothelin receptor signaling in hypercholesterolemic mice. *Proceedings of the National Academy of Sciences* 96: 6920–6924.

42. J. Alper (1999). From the bioweapons trenches, new tools to combat microbes. *Science* 284 (11 June): 1754–1755.

43. Scientific Advisory Board (1997). *New World Vistas: Air and Space Power for the 21st Century* (Human Systems/Biotechnology Volume). Washington, D.C.: United States Air Force.

44. E. Geissler (1995). "What can we learn from BTW history?" Paper presented at the Pugwash Meeting No. 212, Geneva, 2–3 December.

45. J. Jelsma (1995). Military implications of biotechnology. In M. Fransman et al., eds., *The Biotechnology Revolution.* Oxford: Blackwell, pp. 284–297.

46. R. E. Franck, Jr., and G. G. Hildebrandt (1996). Competitive aspects of the contemporary military-technical revolution: Potential rivals to the US. *Defense Analysis* 12, no. 2: 239–258.

47. R. L. Phillips and M. Freeling (1998). Plant genomics and our food supply: An introduction. *Proceedings of the National Academy of Sciences* 95: 1969–1970.

48. D. M. Moore et al. (1998). The African swine fever virus thymidine kinase gene is required for efficient replication in swine macrophages and for virulence in swine. *Journal of Virolology* 72, no. 12: 10310–10315.

49. Commission to Assess the Organization of the Federal Government to Combat the Proliferation of Weapons of Mass Destruction (1999). *Combating Proliferation of Weapons of Mass Destruction.* Pursuant to U.S. Public Law 293, 104th Cong. Washington, D.C.

7

Agent Delivery

The current technological capabilities of the biological and medical community and concerns about their possible misuse in offensive biological warfare programs did not come about by chance, or just recently. The development of modern biology and medicine has long roots; but for present purposes, the major developments can be dated from the latter part of the nineteenth century. There occurred then "one of medicine's few true revolutions: bacteriology. Seemingly resolving age-old controversies over pathogenesis, a new and immensely powerful aetiological doctrine rapidly established itself" (1). Furthermore, and—it appears—rather unusually for medicine, "the new disease theories led directly and rapidly to genuinely effective preventive measure and remedies, saving lives on a dramatic scale" (1).

The impact of the revolution was enormous, driving down infant mortality rates from the 150 or more per thousand that characterized even the industrial world at that time toward the single figure rates of some Western European countries today. Scientists of world standing such as Louis Pasteur in France and Robert Koch in Germany led the way in this golden age of bacteriology in which many of the bacterial diseases that had ravaged human populations—cholera, plague, and so on—were now understood, and effective remedies developed.

A British Royal Army Medical Corps training manual of 1908 described the new thinking succinctly: "[D]iseases like enteric fever, cholera, dysentery, small-pox, plague, malaria and a number of others, all of which are caused by the entering into the body from without of the cause, which is a living thing or germ. It is quite clear that, from the nature of their causation, the various diseases . . . are more or less preventable" (2). In short, specific microorganisms were shown to cause specific diseases in humans, animals, and plants. By attacking these microorganisms, the diseases could be cured or prevented.

As we now know, this new knowledge of disease causation was misused by both sides during World War I in sabotage campaigns aimed at destroying the valuable draft animal stocks of the enemy. This misuse of science was repeated, for example, when new developments such as the proper understanding of viruses (in the 1950s–1960s) and the advent of genetic engineering (in the 1970s–1980s) were misused in the offensive biological warfare program of the former Soviet Union.

AEROBIOLOGY

A particular aspect of these developments that needs to be dealt with here is *aerobiology,* the study of the way in which microorganisms and their toxic products are transported in the air. There were certainly studies of the transport of airborne particles in the nineteenth century, but it is significant that a specialist at the British Chemical Defence Establishment at Porton Down could write in 1987: "That micro-organisms can be spread by aerial transport through rooms, buildings, cities, continents and throughout the atmosphere, now is difficult to refute. . . . In contrast, at the turn of the century, the opposite view was held . . . and was still quite prevalent in the late 1930s" (3). The revised opinion resulted from the increasing development of the science of aerobiology from the 1930s onward.

It is significant that the massive and gruesome Japanese offensive biological weapons program of the 1930s and early 1940s did not lead to effective weaponization of agents. By contrast, Paul Fildes, the leading British microbiologist at the time, quickly determined at the beginning of World War II that "the most effective way would be to disseminate an aerosol of lung-retention sized particles from a liquid suspension of bacteria in a bursting munition such as a bomb delivered so that effective concentrations would be inhaled by anyone in the target area" (4). This approach defined the direction that was then followed by succeeding offensive programs through the rest of the century.

A quantitative scientific study was made within the U.S. program to discover and achieve the best dispersion of agents. We can to some extent follow what was done from the literature of the time. In mid-July 1942 British trials demonstrated that the aerosol cloud that could be produced from bombs containing about 3 liters of anthrax spore suspension was extremely potent, and it was realized that this biological weapon "appeared to be more potent than any CW agent or munition of like size yet examined" (4). In May 1943 all of the data on the British work was transferred to the United States and Canada, as collaborative work got under way (4).

Theodore Rosebury, who in 1949 produced an early popular account of U.S. biological warfare research in World War II, had published a detailed account in 1947 of the technical work carried out by the United States entitled *Experimental Air-Borne Infection* (5, 6). However, Bill Patrick, a senior scientist involved in the postwar U.S. offensive program, stated recently that he had doubts during the 1950s and 1960s about whether biological weapons would actually work (7). These doubts were apparently removed only by a series of major trials in the Pacific during 1968. These trials, involving enough ships to form the world's fifth largest navy, involved testing the effects of aerosol clouds of real agents, including lethal agents, on hundreds of rhesus monkeys loaded onto barges at sea. This account of Patrick's work will be revisited later, particularly as it includes a joint interview with Ken Alibek, the senior Soviet weapons designer who defected to the West in the early 1990s and who, as we saw in Chapter 5, has subsequently been a major source of public information on that program.

Patrick's eventual confidence about the utility of biological warfare was almost certainly also informed by the considerable experimentation done on the airborne survival of agents in the U.S. offensive program in the 1950s and 1960s. Public versions of some of this work became available during the 1960s, at a series of international conferences whose proceedings were published. A first conference in 1960 was followed by a symposium on aerobiology in 1963 (8). The 1963 symposium became known as the First International Conference on Aerobiology. It was followed by a Second International Conference on Aerobiology (Airborne Infection) in 1966, and then by a Third International Symposium, held this time in the UK, in 1970, by which time the U.S. offensive program was coming to an end (9, 10).

The presence of U.S. military scientists was obviously important at all three of these meetings. The first, held at the University of California at Berkeley, was sponsored by the Office of Naval Research, and the proceedings were published by the U.S. Navy. The second conference, held in Chicago, was sponsored by the Illinois Institute of Technology Research Institute and the U.S. Army Biological Center at Fort Detrick. Although the publication resulting from the third meeting was edited by a UK scientist from the Microbiological Establishment at Porton Down, and the meeting was partly supported by the UK Ministry of Defence, numerous U.S. scientists participated. These included a number from military establishments like Fort Detrick. The conferences included contributions on methodological issues of interest to both military and civil scientists, and on issues of clear civil defensive, military medical concern. They also, however, give an indication of the work being carried out on organisms that might possibly be considered for weaponization as biological warfare agents and indeed on organisms that *were* weaponized by the United States. Following are the titles of some of the contributions from the second meeting in 1966:

- Aerogenic Immunization of Man with Live Tularemia Vaccine
- Respiratory Antibody to *Francisella tularensis* in Man
- Antibiotic Prophylaxis and Therapy of Airborne Tularemia
- Infection of Pigeons by Airborne Venezuelan Equine Encephalitis Virus
- Attenuation of Aerosolized Yellow Fever Virus After Passage in Cell Culture
- Aerosol Vaccination with Tetanus Toxoid
- Aerosol Infection of Monkeys with *Rickettsia rickettsii*
- Industrial Inhalation Anthrax
- Epidemiology of Airborne Staphylococcal Infection
- Experimental Epidemiology of Cocciodiomycosis (9)

Though all these contributions are clearly angled at preventive/defensive aspects of research, it has to be noted that tularemia (*Francisella tularensis*), Venezuelan equine encephalitis (VEE) virus, and anthrax were agents actually weaponized in the U.S. offensive program. Moreover, if the papers are examined in more detail, infecting "[h]ealthy young Seventh Day Adventist soldiers" with 25,000 airborne *Francisella tularensis* bacteria and then treating the resulting disease must have furnished information that could be compared with more extensive data obtained by infecting experimental animals (11). Comparing the incidence of industrial inhalation anthrax in human workers and monkeys sampling the same airflow was surely also going to provide information of some value (12). It was presumably input from these and related military studies that led the United Nations and the World Health Organization, in the run-up to the agreement of the Biological and Toxin Weapons Convention in the early 1970s, to issue such dire forecasts about the consequences of using biological weapons, and why official bodies such as the Congress Office of Technology Assessment have continued to do so during the 1990s (13).

Perhaps less well known is a 1992 paper presented by the United States to the ad hoc group (AHG) of governmental experts appointed to identify and examine potential verification measures for the Biological and Toxin Weapons Convention. The research behind this paper was designed to determine what a militarily significant quantity of a toxin might be and then to compare that with the quantities of toxins being used in civil research and medical practice (14). The research made standard assumptions, including that the toxin would be dispersed in air with a 100-meter boundary ceiling, and that people in the region of attack would have a ventilation rate of 12 liters per minute. It was also assumed that a military base would occupy an area of 10 square kilometers and a city or battlefield larger areas of 1,000 and 3,000 square kilometers, respectively. A table was presented (Table 7.1) that indicated the amounts of toxin that would

Table 7.1   Amount of Toxin Required for Lethality in Various Attack Scenarios

Assumptions	Base	City	Battlefield
LD_{50} = 10 ng[a], eff = 1%	1 g	1 kg	3 kg
LD_{50} = 10 ng, eff = 50%	.02 g	20 g	60 kg
LD_{50} = 100 ng, eff = 1%	10 g	10 kg	30 kg

Source: From reference 14.
Note: a. 1 ng = 10^{-9}g (or 0.001 µg).

be needed for various attack scenarios under certain assumptions about the toxicity of the toxin and the efficiency of dispersal of the agent.

The paper concluded: "Even with the conservative assumptions of low toxicity (100 ng per individual) and extremely poor distribution efficiency (1%), a few tens of kilograms of a toxin can contaminate a large battlefield" (14). A paper prepared for the Conference of the Committee on Disarmament in 1970 stated:

> If 15 tons of nerve agent would cause 50 per cent deaths over an area of up to 60 square kilometres, then about one and one-half kilograms of botulinum toxin could *theoretically* produce the same effect. Or, 15 tons of botulinum toxin could theoretically cause 50 per cent deaths in an unprotected population in an area up to 600,000 square kilometres. (15)

The accuracy of this calculation would again depend on the efficiency of distribution. But would an attacker necessarily be limited to very low levels of efficiency of dispersal from weapons systems?

At the time of the 1991 Gulf War, the Iraqis had only relatively crude munitions available. These consisted of a chamber filled with the agent in liquid slurry form, which had a tube filled with explosive placed in its center. At the moment of impact the explosive would detonate and disperse the agent. This system has many drawbacks: Live agents, for one, tend to lose virulence quickly in the slurry; more important, it is difficult to obtain effective production of particles of the correct size to enter and stay in the victims' lungs. One informed commentator suggested in 1997, however, that within a year, the Iraqis could perfect techniques for drying biological warfare agents and could install improved aerosol-forming and disseminating equipment on suitable aircraft (16).

That would not be the end of the process: "Thereafter, remotely piloted vehicles, long-range fighter-bombers, or cruise missiles equipped with tanks and sprayers . . . could . . . disperse agents under conditions favourable for carrying out a successful attack" (16). In this regard, it is well to remember how prevalent the use of aircraft for crop spraying has become around the world (17).

Developing weapons-grade agents and sophisticated delivery systems was the kind of work that members of the U.S. offensive biological warfare program, like Bill Patrick, were engaged in when President Richard Nixon closed the program down in the late 1960s. Ken Alibek received his doctorate of science in 1988 for directing the team that produced the most effective of the former Soviet Union's weapons-grade anthrax agents. This agent, which became operational in 1989, "is an amber-grey powder, finer than bath talc, with smooth, creamy particles that tend to fly apart and vanish in the air, becoming invisible and drifting for miles" (7). The improved material was four times more efficient than the standard material. Anyone who doubts the effectiveness of even the less efficient material would do well to reflect on what we now know of the accident at Sverdlovsk in 1979. There, it seems, an accident in a military test facility allowed the release of a very small amount of anthrax, which nevertheless killed tens of people in the town, despite all the efforts of the medical and government agencies (18, 19).

In considering the potential effectiveness of biological attacks today, we have to take several developments into account. We now have a far greater understanding of the atmosphere and its workings as a result of our tremendously increased capacity for computer modeling. So predicting the weather conditions required for optimal attacks has become much more of a science than an art (20). Similarly, our theoretical understanding of aerosols has developed in order to deal with a wide range of industrial and environmental problems (21). Finally, we now have a rather complete description of how inhaled aerosols behave in the human lung (22).

Although considerable attention has been given to how to deal with an aerosol attack, no one can be satisfied with the imbalance between capabilities for offense and defense at the present time (23). Do current developments in the booming modern biotechnology area have any implications for this imbalance in the future?

DRUG DELIVERY

The revolution in biotechnology has allowed pharmaceutical companies to devise many new and useful medicinal drugs. A major problem, however, is that many of these drugs are peptides and proteins that, if taken orally, are broken down quickly by enzymes in the stomach. This means that some vital medicines, such as insulin for diabetics, have to be taken by regular injection. Injection is a far-from-ideal method of taking a medical product over many years, so drug companies are seeking new delivery methods (24).

One way of introducing chemicals into the body is by inhalation into the lungs. This process occurs on a daily basis in the many people who smoke tobacco and get the nicotine their body craves into their bloodstream. It is perhaps not a surprise, therefore, that one method of drug administration that is being actively explored for good medical reasons is delivery by inhalation. People with asthma, of course, have long used inhalers to administer airway-opening compounds, and in the early 1990s Genentech began to market an aerosol-delivered protein enzyme to break down unwanted DNA in the lungs of cystic fibrosis sufferers. What we are now seeing is an across-the-board range of developments in capabilities for the delivery of drugs by inhalation. This cannot help but have implications for the possibility of delivery of toxins or peptides for malign purposes, too.

Major pharmaceutical companies are simultaneously examining both the development of new drugs and the delivery method because of the advantages to be gained in the market from a good drug with a good delivery system (25). Some companies have their own drug-delivery research centers while others work in cooperation with specialist drug-delivery companies. One new type of development is the delivery of drugs through the skin, as with low doses of nicotine through skin patches to help victims give up tobacco smoking. For drug delivery via the lungs, two examples of developments are pressurized, metered-dose inhalation (MDI) aerosols and the newer, dry powder inhalation (DPI) systems. When thinking about sophisticated drug delivery, however, it is not only the route of drug administration that needs to be considered. Another issue altogether is delivery of a drug, not through a *specific route* but to a *specific target* in the body (26). The matter of delivery to specific targets will be discussed later in the chapter after first examining the specific aerosol route of delivery in more detail.

The difficulty of delivering peptides and proteins to the body by noninvasive means such as ingestion and inhalation is not just because they are easily broken down by enzymes. As well as being susceptible to enzymatic breakdown, they are sensitive to acidic conditions as well. They can also be quite large molecules with an electrical charge and relatively hydrophilic, and thus not easily transported across membranes. So getting such material across the skin, across the lungs into the bloodstream, or across mucous membranes (in the nose, for example) is no easy task. Despite the difficulties, progress is being made and the pulmonary route looks to be the most promising method. Several proteins and peptides are being investigated for delivery by this route. They include insulin and human growth hormone.

Detailed reviews of technological developments show clearly what is regarded as critical for better delivery of drugs by aerosol via the lungs.

For instance, C. Lalor and A. Hickey write: "The physicochemical properties of the aerosols, such as particle size and distribution, density, morphology, hygroscopicity and, in the case of liquids, viscosity, surface tension and evaporation-condensation play a significant role in effective drug delivery and efficacy" (27). It is also clear that considerable progress is expected to be made in understanding and controlling such factors. Lalor and Hickey conclude that the search for systems with optimal therapeutic properties will remain a high priority for pharmaceutical companies and that important, fundamental observations regarding the physicochemical properties of these systems will continue to occur and improve the prospects for future drug delivery to the lungs (27).

From our perspective, any such developments can hardly be irrelevant to the more malign purpose of delivering biological warfare agents through aerosols to the lungs. Ken Alibek's doctor of science degree was presumably awarded because he had found means to better disperse and deliver anthrax spores through an aerosol to the lungs. It should be noted that the equipment needed to produce a freeze-dried and milled *agent* would not differ greatly from that required to freeze-dry and mill *pharmaceutical* material for aerosol delivery. This technical account referred to above suggests, for example, that attrition jet milling "is designed to grind crystalline or friable materials to an average particle size of less than 5 μm without contamination or harm to the product" (27). Moreover, the quantities that can be milled are limited only by the dimensions of the collection vessel and feed hopper. Commercially available attrition mills range in size from those that can just mill gram-sized quantities up to manufacturing units capable of producing kilogram quantities.

One method of achieving better dispersal of an agent in an aerosol that has long been known is to microencapsulate the particles in a protective material, which prevents rapid degeneration in the environment (13). A similar approach can be adopted to protect a drug and prevent its rapid clearance from the blood once it is in circulation. A recent report noted: "Degradable polymer microspheres have also been designed to maintain the systematic levels of peptides such as LHRH [leutinizing hormone release hormone], proteins such as growth hormone (GH) . . . and vaccines such as staphylococcal enterotoxin B" (26).

Considerable commercial success has been reported for the LHRH peptide encapsulated system, and numerous reports exist of similar systems where the active agent is released as the protecting polymer slowly degrades. The development of other such systems into commercial products seems very probable, but, once again, the knowledge is potentially open to misuse. However, even if an agent were to be introduced into the blood system, it would still, in a sense, be passive there—awaiting take-up by the target cells where its effects would be manifested. A much more effective system would be one in which the organ system to be affected was actively targeted.

SPECIFIC TARGETS

Neuropeptides are prominent in the system for transmitting information between neurons of the brain and spinal cord. Thus, one organ system that an attacker might very much wish to attack is the central nervous system. This would be a difficult task, though, for in addition to other problems that would be encountered, the CNS has a special, protective, blood-brain barrier that effectively segregates the brain and spinal cord from the circulating blood and only allows selective movement of materials (28). The fine blood vessels or capillaries surrounding the CNS lack the small pores that in other parts of the body allow the rapid movement of substances into and out of the blood. The capillaries around the central nervous system are lined with tightly aligned special endothelial cells that are sealed together with tight junctions. Furthermore, they are packed with enzymes to degrade any unwanted material that does begin to pass across.

Despite such difficulties, the advantages of being able to deliver medical products directly to the brain has spurred research aimed at finding viable solutions to overcoming the blood-brain barrier (29). One method is to turn a water-soluble active peptide into a derivative with increased lipid solubility. This has more chance of crossing the barrier, and the normal peptide may then be released from its derivative by the action of local enzymes. The derivative of the active peptide thus forms an inactive prodrug during the transport process. In a more sophisticated chemical delivery system, a second chemical group is also attached to the peptide so that when local enzymes release the peptide from its prodrug, the second group remains attached to the peptide and prevents it from moving out of the central nervous system. The material can then be metabolized in the CNS and the active component released in a sustained way.

There are *some* active transport mechanisms that preferentially transport essential metabolites across the blood-brain barrier. An example is the transport of glucose, which is needed in quantity for brain functions. Attempts are being made to design materials that will also be taken up and carried across the barrier by these transport mechanisms.

It has been argued that, in the past, there was an asymmetry between the efforts put into new drug discovery and the discovery of means to deliver the drugs across the blood-brain barrier (30). The result was that many new, potentially useful peptides were being discovered but that only a few were entering the market. It seems likely that the pharmaceutical companies will find ways to rectify that situation and that more effective means of drug delivery, particularly to the brain, will be commercialized in the early years of the twenty-first century.

Of course, with increasing knowledge of the receptors on different cell types, it is now possible to attempt direct targeting of particular kinds of cells. For example, certain types of cancer cells may have characteristics that allow monoclonal antibodies—specific for such cells—to be produced. Much effort has gone into the development of chimeric (hybrid) molecules in which, for example, an active part of a toxin is attached to such a monoclonal antibody. When administered, the monoclonal antibody delivers the toxin specifically to the cancerous cells that need to be killed. In another approach, an enzyme is attached to the monoclonal antibody; after attachment of the enzyme/antibody complex to the target cancer cells, the patient is given a prodrug that the enzyme then converts to an active drug at the site of the cancer (31). With the affinity that neuropeptides have for specific receptor types, by similar methods it is possible to get the peptides to deliver other molecules to specific sites. One example is the use of Substance P in conjunction with the catalytic and transmembrane parts of diphtheria toxin (in a chimeric molecule) as a means of targeting the toxin to cell lines carrying the human receptor for Substance P. The toxin is then converted into its active form and kills these specific cells (32).

Now that it is possible to produce nonpeptide mimics of natural peptides, the pharmaceutical industry may well decide that attempting to deliver peptides as drugs is not the best solution. Indeed, one review of the design of such peptide mimics (or mimetics) argued: "The vision of the future is that one day it will be possible to represent the active sites of all peptides and proteins in the form of orally active small molecule mimetics which are inexpensive to manufacture and convenient to administer" (33).

The review suggested that achievement of that goal is a long way off, but it also suggested that the first steps were being successfully taken. It concluded: "Peptide mimetics technology is advancing at such a rapid pace that the potential is already there to replace many of the recombinant protein products presently on the market with orally active and inexpensive active site mimetics" (33). Of particular interest was the way the field of drug development was anticipated to proceed in the future. The review argued for a new paradigm of drug discovery: "Indeed, in the pharmaceutical world, the field of molecular biology seems destined to become a service industry, providing the medicinal chemist with the biological and structural information necessary for mimetic creation" (33).

Among the peptides for which mimetics were discussed in this review are those that the Canadian document *Novel Toxins and Bioregulators,* prepared for the Third Review of the Biological and Toxin Weapons Convention, considered worthy of discussion: oxytoxin, vasopressin, gonadotropin-releasing hormone (gonadoliberin, LRF), enkephalins, tachykinins (Substance P), endothelins, somatostatin, and neurotensin (34).

The review of the design of peptide mimics ended by suggesting that "the new age of peptide mimetics" would revolutionize the civil industry and its design. Should these kinds of capabilities become available—and it really does seem likely that they will—then similar capabilities would also be available to weapons designers (35). Specifically designed and less fragile, small molecules with greatly enhanced effects could then become agents of choice for some malign purposes. Such a development would appear to significantly diminish the difficulties of agent delivery in the future. Some examples of nonpeptide analogs—antagonists for tachykinin and endothelin receptors, developed for good medical reasons—are presented in Table 7.2.

Table 7.2 Nonpeptide Antagonists

Tachykinin Receptors	Selective Antagonists
NK_1	CP96345, RP67580, SR140333, CP99994
NK_2	SR48968, GR159897
NK_3	SR142801, PD161182, SB223412
Mixed NK_1/NK_2	MDL105212A
Endothelin	Selective Antagonists
ET_A	BMS182874, PD155080, PD156707, TBC11251
ET_B	Ro468443
Mixed ET_A/ET_B	Bosentan, Ro462005, SB209670, L749329

Source: From reference 36.

The next chapter will examine what sorts of purposes the capabilities of these nonpeptide antagonists might be used to achieve.

REFERENCES

1. R. Porter (1997). *The Greatest Benefit to Mankind: A Medical History of Humanity from Antiquity to the Present.* London: HarperCollins.
2. War Office (1908). *Royal Army Medical Corps Training.* London: HMSO.
3. C. S. Cox (1987). *The Aerobiological Pathway of Microorganisms.* Chichester: John Wiley and Sons.
4. G. B. Carter (1992). Biological warfare and biological defence in the United Kingdom 1940–1979. *Journal of the Royal United Services Institute* (December): 67–74.
5. T. Rosebury (1949). *Peace or Pestilence: Biological Warfare and How to Avoid It.* New York: McGraw-Hill.
6. T. Rosebury (1947). *Experimental Air-Borne Infection.* Baltimore, Md.: The Williams and Wilkins Company.
7. R. Preston (1998). The bioweaponeers. *The New Yorker,* March, pp. 52–65.
8. R. L. Dimmick, ed. (1963). *Proceedings of the First International Symposium of Aerobiology.* Oakland, Calif.: Naval Biological Laboratory.
9. E. F. Wolfe, ed. (1966). Second International Conference on Aerobiology (Airborne Infection). *Bacteriological Reviews* 30, no. 3: 485–794.

10. I. H. Silver, ed. (1970). *Aerobiology: Proceedings of the Third International Symposium.* London: Academic Press.

11. W. D. Sawyer et al. (1966). Antibiotic prophylaxis and therapy of airborne tularemia. *Bacteriological Reviews* 30, no. 3: 542–550.

12. P. S. Brachman et al. (1966). Industrial inhalation anthrax. *Bacteriological Reviews* 30, no. 3: 646–659.

13. M. R. Dando (1994). *Biological Warfare in the 21st Century.* London: Brassey's.

14. United States (1992). *Biologically Derived Toxins: Quantities for Legitimate Use.* Ad Hoc Group of Governmental Experts to Identify and Examine Potential Verification Measures from a Scientific and Technical Standpoint. BWC/CONF.III/VEREX/WP.88, Geneva, 4 December.

15. United States (1970). *Working Paper on Toxins.* Conference of the Committee on Disarmament, CCD/286, Geneva, 21 April.

16. R. A. Zilinskas (1997). Iraq's biological weapons: The past as future. *Journal of the American Medical Association* 278, no. 5: 418–424.

17. National Agricultural Aviation Association (1997). *The World of Agricultural Aviation* (Supplement to *Agricultural Aviation*). Wahpeton, N.D.: NAAA.

18. F. A. Abramova et al. (1993). Pathology of inhalation anthrax in 42 cases from the Sverdlovsk outbreak of 1979. *Proceedings of the National Academy of Science* 90: 2291–2294.

19. P. J. Jackson et al. (1998). PCR analysis of tissue samples from the 1979 Sverdlovsk anthrax victims: The presence of multiple *Bacillus anthracis* strains. *Proceedings of the National Academy of Sciences* 95: 1224–1229.

20. M. Z. Jacobson (1999). *Fundamentals of Atmospheric Modeling.* Cambridge: Cambridge University Press.

21. I. Colbeck (1998). Introduction to aerosol science. In I. Colbeck, ed., *Physical and Chemical Properties of Aerosols.* London: Blackie Academic and Professional, pp. 1–30.

22. B. O. Stuart (1973). Deposition of inhaled aerosols. *Archives of Internal Medicine* 131: 60–73.

23. S. L. Wiener (1996). Strategies for the prevention of a successful biological warfare aerosol attack. *Military Medicine* 161, no. 5: 251–256.

24. R. F. Service (1997). Drug delivery takes a deep breath. *Science* 277 (29 August): 1199–1200.

25. K. K. Jain (1998). Strategies and technologies for drug delivery systems. *TiPS* 19 (May): 155–156.

26. D. K. Pettit and W. R. Gombotz (1998). The development of site-specific drug-delivery systems for protein and peptide biopharmaceuticals. *TIBTECH* [Trends in Biotechnology] 16 (August): 343–349.

27. C. B. Lalor and A. J. Hickey (1998). Pharmaceutical aerosols for delivery of drugs to the lungs. In I. Colbeck, ed., *Physical and Chemical Properties of Aerosols.* London: Blackie Academic and Professional, pp. 391–428.

28. N. Bader and P. Buchwald (1998). All in the mind. *Chemistry in Britain* (January): 36–40.

29. L. Prokai (1998). Peptide drug delivery into the central nervous system. *Progress in Drug Research* 51: 95–132.

30. W. M. Pardridge (1994). New approaches to drug delivery through the blood-brain barrier. *TIBTECH* 12 (June): 239–245.

31. F. M. Huennekens (1994). Tumour targeting: Activation of prodrugs by enzyme-monoclonal antibody conjugates. *TIBTECH* 12 (June): 234–239.

32. C. E. Fisher et al. (1996). Genetic construction and properties of a diphtheria toxin-related Substance P fusion protein: In vitro destruction of cells bearing Substance P receptors. *Proceedings of the National Academy of Sciences* 93: 7341–7345.

33. G. J. Moore et al. (1995). Design and pharmacology of peptide mimetics. *Advances in Pharmacology* 33: 91–141.

34. Canada (1991). *Novel Toxins and Bioregulators: The Emerging Scientific and Technological Issues Relating to Verification and the Biological and Toxin Weapons Convention.* Ottawa, September.

35. T. J. Marrone et al. (1997). Structure-based drug design: Computational advances. *Annual Review of Pharmacological Toxicology* 37: 71–90.

36. C. Betancur et al. (1997). Nonpeptide antagonists of neuropeptide receptors: Tools for research and therapy. *TiPS* 18 (October): 372–386.

8

Targets

In late July 1999 the *Washington Post* carried an article with the title "Preparing for a Grave New World" that reported: "In the past year, dozens of threats to use chemical or biological weapons in the United States have turned out to be hoaxes. *Someday one will be real"* (emphasis added) (1). The article asked what that day would look like and gave an alarming account that included the following prediction: "The march of the contagion would accelerate astoundingly, with doctors offering little relief. Hospitals would become warehouses for the dead and the dying. A plague more monstrous than anything we have experienced could spread" (1). The author of the article was particularly concerned about the possibility that some foreign military arsenals might still contain stocks of smallpox virus, a virus that had so devastated human populations in earlier times. It was difficult to ignore the warnings given in this article because the author was William S. Cohen, the U.S. secretary of defense. Furthermore, similar warnings had been given by Defense Department officials to Congress earlier in the year (2).

It is salutary to remember, in this context, how far a country of modest technological capability like Iraq had been able to develop its chemical and biological arsenal prior to 1991. According to a 1998 U.S. Congressional Research Service issue brief, "[t]he Iraqi chemical arsenal has included nerve agents (Sarin and VX), blister agents ('mustard gas') and psychoactive agents (so-called Agent 15). Biological/toxin warfare agents produced by Iraq include anthrax, botulinum, aflatoxins, ebola virus, bubonic and pneumonic plague, ricin and *Clostridium perfringens"* (3). Indeed, 19,000 liters of botulinum toxin were produced, and some of this material was weaponized in 100 botulinum bombs and sixteen missile warheads. According to the report, Iraq also manufactured seven aflatoxin bombs. Aflatoxin toxin is a product of fungi that occur naturally on moldy grain. Why Iraq should have manufactured such a toxin and weaponized it is unclear. The toxin can cause liver cancer in humans, but only after a lapse of decades. In regard to Agent 15, the issue brief reported the British government's recent assertion that Iraq had developed large stocks of this incapacitant. According to the Congressional Research Service: "It is apparently a glycollate similar in effect to the agent BZ. . . . If this is correct, exposure to about 100 milligrams in aerosolized form would be sufficient to incapacitate" (3).

Agents such as BZ and Agent 15 interfere with the operation of neurotransmitters in the central nervous system (4). Symptoms would begin about half an hour after exposure and would last for several days. They would include dizziness, confusion, hallucinations, and others. The United States itself had earlier decided that BZ was too unpredictable in its effects to be used as a battlefield agent.

The evidence on Iraq raises serious questions about exactly what operational plans it had for the possible use of its chemical and biological arsenal prior to 1991. It has to be noted that Iraq was then also beginning research into genetic engineering (5). This research raises a further question of what operational plans Iraq might have had for the *future* use of its chemical and biological weapons. Matthew Meselson, the eminent Harvard biologist who has long been disturbed about the development of biological weapons, presented a concern about possible outcomes in a January 1999 speech to the American Academy of Arts and Sciences. He quoted from a prize-winning article written by a U.S. naval officer in the late 1980s who suggested that "[t]he outlook for biological weapons is grimly interesting. Weaponers have only just begun to explore the potential of the biotechnological revolution. It is sobering to realize that far more development lies ahead than behind" (6). Meselson commented that if this prediction is correct, biotechnology will profoundly change the nature of weapons and the context in which they are employed. At the end of his speech, Meselson warned: "At present, we appear to be approaching a crossroads—a time that will test whether biotechnology, like all major predecessor technologies, will come to be intensively exploited for hostile purposes or whether instead our species will find the collective wisdom to take a different course" (6).

The possibilities for taking that other course will be considered in the remaining two chapters. Here we should note how the offensive biological warfare program of the former Soviet Union illustrates the scale of the change in warfare that could occur if biotechnology is fully applied to offensive warfare. This former Soviet program has not yet been the subject of a full public description, but the most complete account to date is the book by Ken Alibek, a former senior scientist on the program (7). He described, for example, the work carried out in Project Bonfire to use genetic engineering to add a toxin or bioregulator to a pathogenic bacterium. The real interest of Alibek's account lies perhaps not so much in the main text that is organized as a biographical account of his own work, but in the appendices, which list the institutions involved and indicate their main work in the overall program. It seems that the work on weapons targeted at the central and peripheral nervous system under Project Bonfire—in which the toxin added to the pathogenic bacterium destroyed the myelin sheath around nerve cells—was carried out at Obolensk Institute of Applied Microbiology.

If biotechnology is exploited for hostile purposes, it is probably inevitable, given widespread public knowledge of how the human immunodeficiency virus (HIV) attacks the immune system in AIDS, that consideration would be given to attacking the immune system. Human defenses against pathogens have developed with a very complex mechanism. As that mechanism is increasingly understood, the possibility arises not only of "improving" a pathogen's attack but of finding means to degrade the body's immune defenses. Should such an approach be taken, it would be extremely difficult for a defender to diagnose and treat the casualties who might be manifesting many different illnesses caused by a number of different organisms that would opportunistically invade the body, once the normal immune defenses were damaged. In Alibek's list of institutions involved in the Soviet offensive program, it is not surprising to find the Institute of Immunology in Moscow, which, he writes, "[s]tudied regulatory peptides with toxic properties capable of triggering both reversible and irreversible changes in the neural and immune systems" (7). The institute was under the control of the Third Main Directorate of the Ministry of Health—a network of specialist hospitals and medical units that served biological weapons research and development facilities. Within the Ministry of Medical and Microbiological Industries Main Directorate "Biopreparat"—a massive civilian cover operation for advanced military research created in 1973—there was the Lyubychany Institute of Immunology, which "[r]esearched biological agents used to suppress [the] human immune system" (7).

Though Alibek's book gives no further details on this effort to find means of damaging the immune system, there is clearly a great deal of legal civil work being done on immunosuppressants in an attempt to improve the success of organ transplantation. This work had led to the discovery of many new classes of chemicals that can interfere in various ways with the immune system's normal functioning. Among these classes of chemicals are low molecular weight peptides and fragments of peptides. Moreover, "[t]hese low molecular weight peptides . . . provide the basis for development of non-peptide analogues with immunosuppressant activity" (8). Once again it is only to be expected that greater knowledge and more useful compounds will result from this area of research.

Given the enormous scale of agent production and weaponization in the Soviet program during the Cold War, John Steinbruner may have been correct to suggest that "[t]he best guess from what is available on the public record . . . is that Soviet military planners . . . might plausibly have calculated that with judicious selection of agents . . . the urban population of Western Europe might be sufficiently weakened to allow an occupying army to accomplish an otherwise impossible task" (9). That is to say, the Soviet Union might have been intending to use biological weapons in the central military role likely during the Cold War. It is clear, however, that the military could have had a range of other potential uses in mind given the scope of their research and development. We need a wider examination of the possible uses of biological weapons before discussing the operational roles that toxins and bioregulators might be thought to have.

USING BIOLOGICAL WEAPONS

A report on the proliferation of biological weapons, produced by the U.S. Army in 1994, suggested that there are numerous "Concepts of Use" (COUs) for biological weapons and that these can reasonably be grouped into four general types: superpower versus superpower, state versus state, state versus factional element or vice versa, and terrorist use (10). The scope, size, and sophistication of an offensive biological weapons program, in this analysis, are related—at least in a general way—to the concept of use. During the Cold War, the two superpowers each had, at different times, massive offensive biological warfare programs matched to the perceived threat from the other. As would be expected for programs of this size, they were sophisticated and required large-scale equipment and facilities. Humans, animals, and crops were potential targets, and operations could range from delivery of small-scale weapons by simple means to large-scale delivery by highly efficient means. In state versus state conflicts, today the quantities of agents required would be far less than in a superpower/superpower exchange during the Cold War. The programs would therefore be smaller and possibly more difficult to detect. The level of sophistication of the delivery systems would likely be less advanced. Probable targets would be strategic facilities such as ports, airbases, and command posts, but surprise tactical operations against unprotected troops might be attempted.

In a conflict between a state and a factional element, the quantities of agent required would likely be less again and the level of sophistication of the delivery systems could also be much lower. A program focused on classical agents like anthrax and botulinum toxin and crude delivery systems would probably suffice. Tactical applications against unprotected troops and civilian populations could be expected. Besides aerosol attack directed at larger-scale coverage of a target, contamination of food or water supplies might be attempted. Finally, the origin of terrorism could range from a knowledgeable individual working alone to a state-sponsored terrorist organization with substantial resources at its disposal. The quantity and sophistication of the agent and the dispersal system could also range from the simple to the complex. In addition to aerosol attack, agent contamination of food or water supplies would be possible.

This military account of the possibilities adds that one further COU needs to be taken into account. This COU could apply to any of the four conflict situations just described and consists of the use of biological weapons to attack small, strategically important organizational nodes such as communication or command posts. Special forces with capabilities for covert action might be employed; and in small, relatively confined spaces, less toxic agents and smaller quantities of the agent would be required. The potential use of toxins for such an attack is specifically noted.

In a more general analysis, Mark Wheelis has suggested that it is possible to describe the dimensions of biological warfare in terms of the nature of the aggressor, the scale of release of the agent, and the target (11). Within each of these dimensions he suggests that there are three prominent divisions:

1. Nature of the aggressor
   Nations
   Subnational groups
   Individuals
2. Scale of release of the agent
   Point source release
   Medium-scale release
   Large-scale release
3. Target
   Human
   Plants
   Animals (11)

If we consider humans to be the target of attack, then we can see that there are nine possible types of biological warfare, ranging from a point source criminal act by an individual to a large-scale military strategic act by a state (Table 8.1).

Against that background, we can ask where toxins and bioregulators might fit into the thinking about operational planning for biological warfare. However, it is as well to remember that real military planning is a much more complex affair than simply stating how a particular weapon might be used. For instance, by the end of World War I, the British Army had a sophisticated doctrine for the use of its burgeoning chemical weapons arsenal, and this doctrine was fitted carefully into the overall

Table 8.1   Types of Biological Warfare

Scale of Release of the Agent	Nature of the Aggressor		
	Individual	Subnational Group	State
Point source	e.g., Criminal act	e.g., Assassination	e.g., Assassination
Medium scale	e.g., Criminal act	e.g., Terrorist	e.g., Military tactical
Large scale	Not possible	e.g., National liberation	e.g., Military strategic (army) use

Source: From reference 11.

strategy held by the high command for breaking the stalemate on the Western Front. Thus, on the fronts not chosen for the ground attack, chemical weapons were to be used as part of the general process of wearing down the enemy's numbers and morale. Similarly, on the conventional ground attack fronts, prior to assault, chemical weapons were to be used to reduce the enemy's local reserves. However, "at the moment of assault they would change the mission objective to neutralisation, principally counter-battery in order to suppress the enemy's defensive fire and to protect the infantry as they crossed no man's land" (12). When the infantry had reached its objectives, the target of the chemical weapons was to be switched to the enemy rear areas, in order to isolate the battlefield and prevent counterattacks.

Had the war not ended in 1918, the Allies, initially at a disadvantage in chemical warfare because of the strength of the German chemical industry, intended to maximize the advantages they had by then gained. Chemical warfare planners intended to use these weapons on a massive scale to "change the environment of war and create the first truly chemical battlefield" (12). Known deficiencies in the German protective mask, which could not be corrected because of lack of rubber, were to be exploited. The mask itself relied upon "a canister filled with neutralising agents which attached directly to the unit's mouthpiece. This meant that the weight of the drum was borne by the muscles of the wearer's lower face and that it was impractical to increase the size of the canister" (12).

Thus, by applying heavy concentrations of gas, the British intended to overwhelm the capacity of the mask. Furthermore, a new agent, diphenylaminearsine (DM), was to be used, as well as the lethal agents. DM was a sternator (sneezing) agent that could not be neutralized by the German mask. It was an inert chemical that could only be dealt with by further reducing the capacity of the mask by adding a mechanical filter. If this was not done, DM's instant effect on the nose and throat would force the wearer to remove the mask and thus be exposed to the lethal agents.

Had the war continued into 1919, the British chemical warfare planners had in mind an integrated set of plans based on several years of operational experience in deadly warfare, which they expected to cause chaos in the ranks of the enemy. These plans were intended to enhance the success of the military objective of breaking out of the trench warfare stalemate of the previous war years.

AGRICULTURAL WARFARE

It is perhaps surprising, given what we know of its importance in earlier offensive biological warfare programs, that the idea that staple crops might be vulnerable to attack has only recently achieved prominence in the current resurgence of concerns about biological attacks by terrorists (13, 14, 15). During the Cold War, for example, the United States not only used synthetic plant auxins to attack vegetation in Vietnam (see Chapter 2) but also did careful planning for destruction of the staple food crops of its enemies: Wheat was to be destroyed in Russia and rice in China (13).

In the case of attack on China, a major report of 1958, *The Importance of Rice and the Possible Impact of Antirice Warfare,* is in the public record. The agents of choice, 4-fluorophenoxyacetic acid (KF) and related compounds, were effective against cereal species at about the same level of application as agents like 2,4-D and 2,4,5-T were against broad-leaf plants. Additionally, if used alone against rice at certain stages of its development, the agent had no discernible effect for some time. Only as the rice plants approached maturity did it become apparent that the grains were not filling out. The study commented that "the above effects . . . would be extremely difficult, if not impossible, for the enemy farmer to detect or to anticipate that his rice crop would fail . . . or for that matter, to realize that his crop had even been attacked" (16).

Extensive studies were carried out on rice plants, their cultivation, and the consumption and pattern of trade in rice, as a background to the discussion of the agents that might be used to attack this crucial staple crop. How attacks might be carried out with available weapons and delivery systems—to achieve the desired quantitative reductions in production and therefore possible consumption—was also described. The report concluded, in part, that "[a]t the recommended use rate of 0.5 pounds per acre . . . applied during the susceptible period of rice, the yield may be reduced 50 to 100 per cent. Thus, a loss of 336 to 672 metric tons of rough rice per square mile may be expected" (16). This would be enormously damaging to the most productive growing regions. The report also concluded that "[b]ecause of its potential, a capability to wage antirice warfare is desirable and it is recommended that such a capability be obtained" (16).

OPERATING WITH TOXIN WEAPONS

Against that kind of tough realist background, can we say anything about why toxins (and bioregulators) might be considered useful in a military arsenal, particularly as antipersonnel agents? The U.S. Army's *Biological Warfare Threat Study* of 1983 set out the arguments (17). The study argues that toxins have *several* properties that indicate their potential for use as warfare agents. The first of these are their potency and rapidity of action. The rapidity of action is stated to vary from several seconds to several hours, depending on the type of toxin. The second feature noted is the specificity of action of these agents. (We shall return to this point shortly.) The third feature noted is the stability of certain toxins as compared to standard chemical weapons agents. Moreover, the report states, the stability of some of these compounds indicates that they could be disseminated either by explosive means (i.e., artillery or bombs) or by nonexplosive means (aircraft spray, aerosol generators, etc.) (17). So these agents have versatile potential for very different kinds of use.

In general terms, biological weapons like toxins and bioregulators share with all chemical and biological weapons the potential for causing extreme psychological stress in response to their use because of the unfamiliarity of the threat they pose (18). This would apply just as much to the use of bioregulators of a less lethal kind as to highly lethal toxins. Of course, the speed of action of these chemical toxins and bioregulators as opposed to the relative slowness of action of live pathogens—requiring multiplication of the infective agent in the victim prior to its exerting an effect—would argue for the preferential use of toxins and bioregulators where a speedy result was required.

However, of particular interest here, given the International Committee for the Red Cross's suggestion that what is of concern is the likely development of weapon systems with *specific* damaging effects on particular body organs and functions (Chapter 6), is the specificity of targeting that may become possible. We have seen in the *Biological Warfare Threat Study* that toxins are currently regarded as weapons with important special characteristics. Furthermore, we know that the offensive biological weapons program of the former Soviet Union included Project Bonfire, which involved the introduction of an agent, specifically directed at a key component of the nervous system, into a carrier organism for protection on its way to the victim and to confuse the diagnosis of its effect. Unfortunately, that kind of sophisticated agent development is but the first step along the road to ever more dangerous biological weapons. Professor Meselson is correct: We are at a crossroads, and if we take the wrong path we may see many decades of development of increasingly sophisticated and specifically targeted new biological weapons.

Of course, the kinds of weapons that might be produced and used would be relevant to the wars of the twenty-first century. Given the awful history of ethnic warfare in the twentieth century, it is a sad thought that we shall almost certainly see more interethnic warfare in the next. Many of these conflicts were held in check by the superpowers' rivalry during the Cold War, but they may well continue to surface over the next decades. It has often been suggested that biological weapons could be developed that would be specific for a particular ethnic group. In conditions of long-term and bitter ethnic conflict, there might be the motivation to develop such weapons. This would surely be the ultimate in specificity for a bioweapon-eer—a weapon that would only kill or incapacitate the enemy. What is the possibility that such a fearful weapon might be developed?

ETHNIC WEAPONS

An attack on a particular ethnic group using biological weapons need not necessarily be a sophisticated attack. It could be as crude an assault as using a toxin weapon on an ethnic group. It has been suggested, for example, that Iraq was interested in aflatoxin as a means of causing long-term damage to its Kurdish population by mixing the toxin with riot control agents (19). That this was the intent of the assault would not be detectable until decades later when large numbers of people began to develop liver cancer. Another relatively crude method of assault on an ethnic group would be for an attacker to use a pathogen or toxin that its own troops had been vaccinated against but the victims had not.

What we are discussing here is the possibility of attack on an ethnic group based on its particular genetic characteristics. One example, known for many years, is that different ethnic groups show genetic variation in the frequency of the various blood groups in their populations (20). As we saw in Chapter 6, pharmaceutical companies have a great interest in genetic differences, which lead to drugs being metabolized in different ways; such differences in enzyme function are also sometimes characteristic of different human groups (21). Human infants, for instance, are able to use the lactose in milk because an enzyme called lactase breaks down this sugar. At weaning, the level of lactase decreases sharply in many infants in some populations, but in other populations few infants exhibit this drastic change in the enzyme level. This characteristic is hereditary; it can be tested for easily, and the differences between adult populations can be tabulated (Table 8.2).

Table 8.2 Lactose Absorption by Adult Population

Population	Percentage of Lactose Absorbers
Czechs	100.0
Danes	98.0
Tuaregs (Africa)	85.0
Blacks (United States)	25.0
Eskimos (Greenland)	15.0
Aborigines (Australia)	15.0
Asians (United States)	3.0
Kungs (Africa)	2.5
Bantus (Africa)	0.0

Source From reference 21.

It is also well known that certain major, genetically determined (heredi-tary) diseases occur at different frequencies in different ethnic groups (22). Some representative examples are shown in Table 8.3.

Table 8.3 Some Racial/Ethnic Differences in Single-Gene Disorders

Group	Relatively High Frequency	Relatively Low Frequency
Ashkenazic Jews	Tay-Sachs disease	Phenylketonuria
Mediterranean peoples	Thalassemia (mainly beta)	Cystic fibrosis (CF)
Africans	Alpha and beta thalassemias	CF, phenylketonuria
Chinese	Alpha thalassemia G6PD deficiency (a blood disorder)	HbE (a blood disorder)

Source: From reference 22.

Obviously, if such a genetic difference were very large, it might be possi-ble to target, say, a particular cellular receptor characteristically present in the majority of the ethnic group under attack but little evident in the at-tacker's population. However, a much wider range of possibilities would surely arise if the hereditary material itself—the DNA of the genome—could be targeted.

To see how this might be possible, we need to consider the structure of the human genome in more detail. All cells of the body contain a nu-cleus, within which are chromosomes containing vast lengths of DNA that carry the hereditary information that directs the cells' functions. The DNA incorporates a (triplet) code that directs the eventual production of the key proteins of the body, as has been outlined earlier. The triplet code is car-ried in a small set of chemicals (called nucleotides or nucleotide bases), and because the DNA is double-stranded, the corresponding chemicals in the paired strands are referred to as *base pairs*. The *majority* of the human genome is carried within the nucleus and is about 3 billion base pairs long. A small amount of DNA is carried separately in the energy-generating mitochondria (23). Surprisingly, the approximately 80,000 chromosomal genes that actually code for functional products make up very little of the vast length of DNA, and even within these genes there are long stretches of noncoding DNA. Much of human DNA is made up of long stretches of noncoding sequences of no known function. Other parts consist of a variety of repetitive sequences and pseudogenes that are no longer functional.

What is particularly interesting about the flood of new data that has been produced on DNA sequences is that it has changed our "model" of genes and their mutation. It used to be thought that a single normal gene mutates at *one* point in its sequence to a single mutant-type gene, which causes the disease we see. As discussed in previous chapters, such a change in the gene DNA would cause a change in the protein produced by the gene, a change that could damage the function of the protein. More recently, investigations of the fine structure of genes, like that for cystic fibrosis, show that a mutation can occur at *many* different points along the gene and lead to a malfunctioning gene—and so cause the disease we call cystic fibrosis by disrupting the gene in different ways (24). In fact, most genes have been found to occur in many different forms (or alleles) caused by such different mutations in the gene sequence. Moreover, these changes persist in the DNA sequences of descendants. Because most people throughout history have not moved far in their lifetimes, these characteristic changes tend to be geographically localized (25). Therefore, those changes in DNA sequence that occur as a result of a mutation in noncoding regions of the genome will also persist and characterize localized descendant populations.

The human species probably originated about 100,000 to 200,000 years ago and has not had time to further differentiate into subspecies. Current evidence is that the Neanderthals who lived in Europe from 300,000 to 30,000 years ago, and with whom we must have coexisted for an extended period, have sufficiently different DNA to be regarded as a separate species (26). However, though the human race remains one species, it seems that there is enough variation between different ethnic groups for them to be differentiated by their DNA, particularly if several differences (markers) in the DNA are considered (27). The number of markers is set to grow quite rapidly because of interest from the pharmaceutical companies. Single nucleotide polymorphisms (SNPs) arise from the change of just one base in the DNA sequence. As indicated above, these can occur within a gene or outside of a gene. There are several hundred thousand such single changes, and an effort is now under way to build up a computer databank of 3 million such SNPs. This will provide a tool for the design of drugs that do not cause unexpected and unwanted reactions in different individual patients (28).

If we assume that it will become increasingly possible to distinguish between ethnic groups on the basis of DNA markers, what else would be needed, say, to have a toxin or abnormal bioregulator produced in that specific group? At a minimum, it would surely be necessary to understand a great deal more about the structure and function of the human genome. It would also be necessary to have means of interfering with the function of the genome in a relatively specific way. That such capabilities may not be impossible to achieve was made clear in the UK contribution to the background paper on scientific and technological developments prepared for the 1996 Fourth Review Conference of the Biological and Toxin Weapons Convention. It stated, in part:

> It is predicted that the human genome will be sequenced by the year 2005. The information is expected to lead to radical new treatments for a broad range of human diseases. . . . It cannot be ruled out that information from such genetic research could be considered for the design of weapons targeted against specific ethnic or racial groups. (29)

The Human Genome Project is certainly the most important single project in biology and medicine today. The project will bring complete knowledge of the structure of the human genome in the early years of the twenty-first century, and that is seen as a starting point for a new effort: to make such structural genomics the basis for a new functional genomics (30, 31). As can be seen from the goals set out in Table 3.1, the HGP will certainly provide advanced capabilities for manipulating the human genome.

So what then of capabilities for interfering with genome function in specific ways? Early expectations for gene therapy as a means of correcting genetic defects in diseases like cystic fibrosis, or of curing cancer by correcting malfunctioning genes, may have had to be lowered because of the many difficulties encountered, but where does the technology stand today? As a background to answering the first of those questions, it is necessary to remember that viruses have evolved to enter cells and alter their functions in just such specific ways. They can only exist by entering living cells and taking over the cellular machinery in order to reproduce themselves. So we are not attempting to do something that has never happened before. Despite the setbacks and disappointed hopes, fundamental and applied work on gene therapy continues. The consolidation of knowledge can be seen, for example, in the understanding we now have of the advantages and disadvantages of various viral and nonviral vector systems.

Among the advantages, we know that *RNA viruses,* which are now being used in the majority of clinical trials, can enter many cell types and carry out gene transfer by integrating stably into the host cell genome (32). The disadvantages include the difficulties of getting efficient delivery into target cells, the inability to infect (and thereby introduce genes into) nondividing cells, and the difficulty of getting sustained, long-term expression of the inserted gene. *DNA adenoviruses,* on the other hand, can transfer genes to a wide variety of cell types, including nondividing cells, and can be manufactured in large quantities. Yet they do not integrate stably into the host cell genome and therefore require repeated administration, during which they can provoke strong immune (rejection) responses.

To answer the second question—of where the technology stands today— the present situation is that as fundamental research continues to improve the capabilities for tackling the difficult diseases that were first envisaged, applied research is turning to simpler problems more fitted to current capabilities. One recent review noted: "Much of the excitement today is from recent developments that apply existing technology to more tractable clinical problems that may not be subject to the limitations of present vectors" (33). Researchers are trying to achieve gene expression that results in production of modest amounts of secreted gene products in readily accessible cells for short periods of time, where that limited output is likely to have a clinically useful effect (34).

The UK was correct to conclude in 1996 that ethnic weapons could not be ruled out. The UK was also correct, *at that time,* in concluding that it was "far from clear that the development of such weapons will ever be anything more than a theoretical possibility" (34). How much longer that conclusion will hold is uncertain. Evidence seems to suggest the continued development—for valid medical reasons, of course—of the necessary capabilities. There is no sign of a significant overall problem that could make ethnic weapons an impossibility.

With the current rate of change in biotechnology and molecular medicine, and should offensive biological weapons programs get out of control, in twenty to fifty years' time we may well be looking at some frightening possibilities. The knowledge may then be available to make the targeting of a particular population group—with a specific vector to achieve some specific malign alteration of specific cells—a possibility. Any such activity would, of course, be illegal under the Genocide Convention, which was agreed and came into force soon after the terrible genocides of World War II (35). As we have seen since, it has not yet been sufficient to prevent genocide. Can the Biological Weapons Convention be strengthened to do better—to prevent the further development of offensive biological weapons programs, and, specifically, to prevent the potential misuse of toxins and bioregulators we have just discussed?

REFERENCES

1. W. S. Cohen (1999). Preparing for a grave new world. *Washington Post,* 26 July, p. A19.

2. P. Mann (1999). Bio-warfare called "weapon of choice." *Aviation Week and Space Technology*, 12 April, pp. 68–69.

3. S. Bowman (1998). *Iraqi Chemical and Biological (CBW) Capabilities.* CRS issue brief. Washington, D.C.: Congressional Research Service.

4. M. R. Dando (1996). *A New Form of Warfare: The Rise of Non-Lethal Weapons.* London: Brassey's.

5. C. Seelos (1999). Lessons from Iraq on bioweapons. *Nature* 398 (18 March): 187–188.

6. M. Meselson (1999). "The problem of biological weapons." Paper presented to the 18th stated meeting of the American Academy of Arts and Sciences, Boston, 13 January.

7. K. Alibek and S. Handelman (1999). *Biohazard.* New York: Random House.

8. B. Kundu and S. K. Khare (1999). Recent advances in immunosuppressants. *Progress in Drug Research* 52: 1–52.

9. J. D. Steinbruner (1998). Biological weapons: A plague upon all houses. *Foreign Policy* (winter): 85–95.

10. R. O. Spertzel et al. (1994). *Biological Weapons Proliferation.* DNA-MIPR-90-715, U.S. Army Medical Research Institute of Infectious Diseases, Fort Detrick, Detrick, Md.

11. M. Wheelis (1997). "'Addressing the full range of biological warfare in a BWC compliance protocol." Paper presented at Pugwash Meeting No. 229, Geneva, 20–21 September.

12. A. Palazzo (1999). Plan 1919—The other one. *Journal of the Society for Army Historical Research* 77: 39–40.

13. S. Whitby and P. Rogers (1997). Anti-crop biological warfare—Implications of the Iraqi and US programs. *Defense Analysis* 13, no. 3: 303–318.

14. P. Rogers, S. Whitby, and M. R. Dando (1999). Biological warfare against crops. *Scientific American* (June): 70–75.

15. S. Goldstein (1999). U.S. could face new terror tactic: Agricultural warfare. *The Inquirer* (Philadelphia), 22 June, pp. 1–4.

16. C. E. Minarik et al. (1958). *The Importance of Rice and the Possible Impact of Antirice Warfare.* Technical Study 5. Biological Warfare Laboratories, Fort Detrick, Detrick, Md.

17. USACMLS Threat Section (1983). *Biological Warfare Threat Study.* U.S. Army Chemical School, Fort McClellan, Alabama, 6 October.

18. J. W. Stokes and L. E. Banderet (1997). Psychological aspects of chemical defense and warfare. *Military Psychology* 9, no. 4: 395–415.

19. J. R. Smith (1997). Playing hide-and-seek with Iraq's warheads. *International Herald Tribune,* 22–23 November, p. 2.

20. A. E. Mourant (1983). *Blood Relations: Blood Groups and Anthropology.* Oxford: Oxford University Press.

21. M. R. Cummings (1994). *Human Heredity: Principles and Issues.* St. Paul, Minn.: West Publishing Company.

22. A. P. Palednak (1989). *Racial and Ethnic Differences in Disease.* Oxford: Oxford University Press.

23. T. A. Brown (1999). *Genomes.* Oxford: BIOS Scientific Publishers.

24. J. Bertranpetit and F. Calafell (1996). Genetic and geographical variability in cystic fibrosis: Evolutionary considerations. In K. M. Weiss, ed., *Variation in the Human Genome.* Chichester: John Wiley and Sons, pp. 9–118.

25. K. M. Weiss (1996). Is there a paradigm shift in genetics? Lessons from the study of human diseases. *Molecular Phylogenetics and Evolution* 5, no. 1: 259–265.

26. M. Krings (1997). Neanderthal DNA sequences and the origin of modern humans. *Cell* 90: 19–30.

27. M. D. Shriver et al. (1997) Ethnic-affiliation estimation by use of population-specific DNA markers. *American Journal of Human Genetics* 60: 957–964.

28. D. Bonn (1999). International consortium SN(i)Ps away at individuality. *The Lancet* 353 (15 May): 1684.

29. United Kingdom (1996). *Background Paper on New Scientific and Technological Developments Relevant to the Convention on the Prohibition of the Development, Production and Stockpiling of Bacteriological (Biological) and Toxin Weapons and on Their Destruction.* Fourth Review Conference, BWC/CONF.IV/4, 30 October, p. 10.

30. F. S. Collins et al. (1998) New goals for the US Human Genome Project: 1998–2000. *Science* 282 (23 October): 682–689.

31. E. S. Lander (1996). The new genomics: Global views of biology. *Science* 274 (25 October): 536–539.

32. W. French Andersen (1998). Human gene therapy. *Nature* 392 (Supplement, 30 April): 25–30.

33. A. E. Smith (1999). Gene therapy—Where are we? *The Lancet* 354 (Molecular Medicine Supplement, July): 1–4.

34. E. G. Nabel (1999). Delivering genes to the heart—right where it counts! *Nature Medicine* 5, no. 2: 141–142.

35. E. J. Osmańczyk (1990). Genocide Convention. *The Encyclopedia of the United Nations and International Relations.* London: Taylor and Francis.

9

Can the Biological and Toxin Weapons Convention Be Strengthened?

P oison has a long history of use in warfare; its use has been abhorred just as long. This revulsion began to be codified in the nineteenth century as part of a general move to prevent the worst excesses of increasingly industrialized warfare. The Lieber Code, drafted during the U.S. Civil War, has an article that states: "The use of poison in any manner, be it to poison wells, or food, or arms, is wholly excluded from modern warfare. He that uses it puts himself out of the pale of law and usages of war" (1).

The international declaration concerning the laws and customs of war, which was signed in Brussels in 1874, and the First and Second Hague Peace Conferences of 1899 and 1907 all reached conclusions about specific prohibitions on poison weapons. In the classic account *CBW and the Laws of War*, produced as part of a Stockholm International Peace Research Institute series in the 1970s, it was argued that the records of the Brussels Conference showed that "in 1874 the reference to poison and poisoned weapons was meant to include the spreading of disease on enemy territory" (2). This, the SIPRI account noted, was also reflected in the wording of the United States Army Manual of 1914, but nevertheless, both chemical and biological warfare were used during World War I.

Following that war, the Geneva Protocol of 1925 instituted what has become a customary international legal prohibition on the use of chemical weapons and, as a result of the intervention of the Polish delegate, on the use of biological weapons as well. The ban embodied in the protocol is extremely general and sweeping.

Protocol for the Prohibition of the Use in War of Asphyxiating, Poisonous or other Gases, and of Bacteriological Methods of Warfare. Signed at Geneva on 19th June 1925.

The Undersigned Plenipotentiaries, in the name of their respective Governments,

Whereas the use in war of asphyxiating, poisonous or other gases, and of all analogous liquids, materials or devices, has been justly condemned by the general opinion of the civilized world; and

Whereas the prohibition of such use has been declared in Treaties to which the majority of the Powers of the world are Parties; and

To the end that this prohibition shall be universally accepted as a part of International Law, binding alike the conscience and the practice of nations;

Declare:

That the High Contracting Parties, so far as they are not already Parties to Treaties prohibiting such use, accept this prohibition, agree to extend this prohibition to the use of bacteriological methods of warfare and agree to be bound as between themselves according to the terms of this declaration. (2)

As was noted in the SIPRI account, "the use of *biological* agents against plants and animals is undoubtedly prohibited by the protocol. This results, first, from the extreme generality of the expression 'bacteriological *methods of warfare*,' which, as regards the target of attack, does not leave room for any restrictive interpretation" (2).

However, the nature of this agreement and the reservations entered by many states essentially reduced it to a *no-first-use agreement*. It certainly did not outlaw research, development, or production of biological and toxin weapons, and it is now clear that a number of states proceeded to do those very things in the interwar period and during World War II. Nevertheless, within the League of Nations system, considerable efforts were made to find better means of restricting such weapons.

Following World War II, chemical and biological weapons came to be classed along with nuclear weapons as weapons of mass destruction. In the decades following the war, despite various accusations of the use of chemical and biological weapons, little real effort went into finding an arms control mechanism for dealing with these weapons, that is, until the large-scale use of nonlethal chemical riot control agents and herbicides by the United States in Vietnam.

The process began with a British proposal in 1968 to deal separately with biological weapons. This initially met with resistance, but it eventually led to the agreement of the Biological and Toxin Weapons Convention in the early 1970s. The BTWC entered into force in 1975, but unfortunately, another two decades were to pass before the Chemical Weapons Convention was also agreed. The BTWC was hailed as a major disarmament achievement that outlawed a whole class of weapons. However, it contained no adequate means of verifying that the state parties were living up to their obligations (3). Following is a summary of the article titles contained in the BTWC:

1. Not to Develop, Produce, Stockpile or Acquire Agents, Weapons, etc.
2. To Destroy Stocks
3. Not to Transfer or Assist Others
4. To Take National Measures
5. To Consult and Cooperate in Solving Problems
6. May Lodge Complaints with the Security Council
7. To Provide Assistance in the Event of a Violation
8. No Detraction from the Geneva Protocol
9. Obliged to Continue Negotiations on Chemical Weapons
10. Cooperate for Peaceful Purposes
11. Amendment
12. Review
13, 14, 15. Duration, Signature, Ratification, Deposition, Languages (3)

Subsequently, this deficiency has been increasingly viewed as a dangerous omission because the biotechnology genomics revolution has raised the potential military significance of these weapons. The BTWC is subject to reviews approximately every five years by the state parties; and, as a result of the kind of detailed considerations reviewed in Chapter 3, efforts have been made to increase the effectiveness of the convention. At the Second Review Conference in 1986 a series of confidence-building measures were agreed. These annual data exchanges were extended at the Third Review Conference in 1991, but it is generally accepted that they have been a failure because few countries have regularly submitted adequate information.

At the Third Review Conference in 1991 it was also agreed to establish a group of government experts to assess whether it was scientifically and technically feasible to strengthen the BTWC through the introduction of some potential verification measures (4). This group of experts and the process that it carried out became known as VEREX. The VEREX group reported positively, and at a Special Conference in 1994 the state parties issued a mandate to a new group of representatives to negotiate a verification protocol to the convention. The work of this Ad Hoc Group continues, with the twentieth session scheduled for late 2000. The AHG has, in fact, been elaborating the text of a protocol since mid-1997, and it is therefore possible to discuss the likely shape of the measures that may be agreed prior to the Fifth Review Conference in 2001.

Mandate of the Ad Hoc Group

The Conference also recognized that the complex nature of the issues pertaining to the strengthening of the Biological Weapons Convention underlined the need for a gradual approach towards the establishment of a coherent regime to enhance the effectiveness of and improve compliance with the Convention. *This regime would include, inter alia, potential verification measures, as well as agreed procedures and mechanisms for their efficient implementation and measures for the investigation of alleged use. . . .*

The objective of this Ad Hoc Group shall be to consider appropriate measures, including possible verification measures, and draft proposals to strengthen the Convention, to be included, as appropriate, in a legally binding instrument, to be submitted for the consideration of the States Parties. In this context, the Ad Hoc Group shall, *inter alia* consider:

- Definitions of terms and objective criteria . . .
- The incorporation of existing and further enhanced confidence building and transparency measures . . .
- A system of measures to promote compliance with the Convention, including, as appropriate, measures identified, examined and evaluated in the VEREX Report . . .
- Specific measures designed to ensure effective and full implementation of Article X . . .

Measures should be formulated and implemented in a manner designed to protect sensitive commercial proprietary information and legitimate national security needs.

Measures shall be formulated and implemented in a manner designed to avoid any negative impact on scientific research, international cooperation and industrial development. (4)

The difficulties of verification in relation to chemical and particularly biological weapons are not trivial. They derive from the fact that the production techniques are fundamentally "dual-use," that is, applicable to both civil and military purposes. A U.S. Army document produced at the height of the U.S. offensive biological weapons program in 1961 specifies the problem:

Much of this research necessary for the development of biological weapons is closely associated with and virtually indistinguishable from public health or academic research. Nearly all work on vaccines and immunology could be justified under public health activities. Studies of aerosols could be of academic interest or they could relate to hospital aerosol infection or to aerogenic vaccination for the efficient immunization of population groups. (5)

This last point is clearly evident in the conference topics related to aerobiology that were discussed during the 1960s, as we saw in Chapter 7. In the view expressed in the U.S. Army document, the difficulties do not end there: "Engineering aspects of the research and development effort could also be performed within the framework of legitimate industrial research, viz., mass culture processes could be developed under legitimate industrial fermentations" (5). Against that background, the long-term skepticism in U.S. circles about the possibility of effective verification for the BTWC is understandable.

The consequences of the biotechnology revolution have exacerbated these difficulties in a number of ways. As early as the Second Review Conference in 1986, the state parties to the BTWC had noted that toxins might be more easily produced by these modern methods in militarily significant quantities. Moreover, the quantities of toxins being used for good medical reasons were also beginning to increase as new uses were discovered. By 1994 Jonathan Tucker, in an extended review of the dual-use problem in relation to toxins in particular, was reporting that "[w]orldwide consumption of toxins for medical therapy and scientific research has increased from a few grams to the current level of hundreds of grams per year, and the projected future growth of toxin therapies will require tens to hundreds of kilograms annually" (6). That growth, he concluded, necessarily blurred the distinction between medically usable and militarily significant quantities of particular toxins.

THE GENERAL PURPOSE CRITERION
AND ITS IMPLEMENTATION

The way the negotiators found around this dual-use problem, for both the Biological and Toxin Weapons Convention and the Chemical Weapons Convention, was to develop a "General Purpose Criterion." Article I of the BTWC states:

> Each State Party to this Convention undertakes never in any circumstances to develop, produce, stockpile or otherwise acquire or retain:
> Microbial or other biological agents, or toxins, whatever their origin or method of production, *of types and in quantities that have no justification for prophylactic, protective or other peaceful purposes.* (emphasis added) (1)

The part of the article emphasized above is the General Purpose Criterion, which makes clear that all biological agents and toxins that have no justification for peaceful purposes are banned. In the later Chemical Weapons Convention, the basic prohibition is again set out in Article I: "Each State Party to this Convention undertakes never under any circumstances: a. To develop, produce, otherwise acquire, stockpile or retain chemical weapons, or transfer directly or indirectly, chemical weapons to anyone" (7). Chemical weapons are defined in Article II as "[t]oxic chemicals and their precursors, *except where intended for purposes not prohibited under the Convention, as long as the types and quantities are consistent with such purposes"* (emphasis added) (7). Again, the part of Article II emphasized above is the General Purpose Criterion. All chemicals are captured by this criterion because in the convention a toxic chemical is defined as "[a]ny chemical which through its chemical action on life processes can cause death, temporary incapacitation or permanent harm to humans or animals" (7). The peaceful purposes that *are* allowed are defined in a further article of the convention.

Thus, it can be seen that the CWC is considerably more developed than the BTWC. This would be expected, given the two decades that elapsed (1975–1997) between the entry into force of the two conventions. However, there are also considerable differences between the civil industries that could facilitate misuse. The chemical industry is a widespread and quite mature industry, whereas the modern biotechnology industry is heavily concentrated in the developed world and subject to massive innovative change. Added to these differences in the industrial base, much larger quantities of chemical agents than biological agents are required for real military significance. Thus, it is to be expected that the ways in which the two conventions are implemented will be likely to differ, despite the same underlying principles operating.

IMPLEMENTING THE CWC

The General Purpose Criterion is implemented in the CWC not by the international organization attempting to monitor all toxic chemicals but by it concentrating on those considered most dangerous. Therefore, the CWC has an extensive but not completely exhaustive list of such chemicals in its series of schedules. Schedule 1 includes known chemical warfare agents and their precursors that have little legitimate civilian use; Schedule 2 lists toxic chemicals and precursors that are used in small quantities for legitimate purposes; and Schedule 3 covers toxic chemicals that currently have widespread civil use. There is also a mechanism that allows the lists to be modified in the light of new technological developments.

The CWC imposes extremely strict limits on the amount of Schedule 1 chemicals that may be produced by a state in any one year and then progressively less stringent restrictions on Schedule 2 and Schedule 3 chemicals. Of course, because some states such as the United States and former Soviet Union held large amounts of chemical weapons prior to the CWC agreement, there is also a requirement for these stocks and the associated manufacturing facilities to be destroyed. The convention works, essentially, by the state parties making annual declarations of their activities in relation to the scheduled chemicals and then through the checking of these declarations for accuracy by the CWC organization in routine visits. There is also a provision for challenge inspections to be made by the organization if there is a well-founded suspicion that illegal activity is occurring in the territory of a state party.

This is the system by which the CWC covers toxins. As Jonathan Tucker has noted, there was extensive discussion during the negotiations about putting botulinum toxin on the list of scheduled chemicals, but its extensive civil uses made this impossible. Eventually, botulinum toxin was left out of the schedules, and "[s]axitoxins and ricin were intended as 'placeholders' to ensure that the CWC's verification regime covers toxins at least until comparable monitoring measures can be implemented for the B[T]WC" (8). Placing saxitoxin and ricin on the Schedule 1 list means that any facility that produces, processes, or consumes more than 100 grams of either toxin per year must be declared and undergo routine inspection. Moreover, production of either toxin at any one facility must not exceed 10 kilograms per year. As we saw in Chapter 4, restrictions on the transfer of these agents have already caused difficulties with regard to enabling proper civil uses of saxitoxin. The latest information suggests that despite such difficulties, the Chemical Weapons Convention is beginning to be implemented in a satisfactory manner (9). But if toxins (and bioregulators) are really to be more appropriately covered by the BTWC, what is—or should be—the shape of the verification regime being designed for that convention in the current negotiation of a verification protocol?

IMPLEMENTING THE BTWC

It has been suggested that the BTWC is "orders of magnitude more difficult to monitor than nuclear, chemical, or conventional arms control accords" (10). It is widely accepted that chemical weapons are most closely related to biological weapons because, for example, both involve the aerosolization of agents in significant military operations. However, the view that there are orders of magnitude of difference between the task facing the BTWC and the task facing the CWC suggests that the dual-use problem in regard to biotechnology is different *in kind* from that in regard to chemical technology. This is untrue; although there are certainly differences in the details between the two cases, there are also similarities (8). In fact, in its overall structure, the problem of verification in the BTWC is directly analogous to that in the CWC. While the CWC does list chemicals in schedules, and links the strictness of monitoring to the schedules, there are many chemicals *not* on the schedules that could be used as chemical weapons. This is particularly true if requirements such as the need for long-term stability or binary mixing just prior to dispersal are dropped. Thus, the CWC schedules are merely *illustrative lists* related to the General

Purpose Criterion, as will also be the case in the BTWC. The fact that there are quantitative limits in the CWC that will likely not be in the BTWC is a red herring. The significant point is that a chemical weapons agent that is not on a schedule could be made on a chemical production line that is not required to be declared or monitored. Verification, confidence, and trust do not come about in the CWC because *all* relevant items can be counted. This will also be the case with the BTWC. The questions therefore are these: What can be used from the developed CWC system? and, What modifications need to be made to meet the particular circumstances of biological weapons monitoring?

A number of authors have considered what a proliferator would need to do to acquire a biological weapons capability (11, 12). They argue that a proliferator would need to go through a series of stages to obtain a significant military capability. The stages for acquiring biological weapons are:

1. Policy review and decision to initiate an offensive program
2. Budgetary estimates and resource allocation
3. Research and development
4. Agent production
5. Design, test, and build munitions
6. Acquire delivery systems
7. Acquire operational capability: develop battle plans; train troops to use BW; integrate weapons, logistics, and plans into military forces (11, 12)

Now, on the one hand, the further down this list of stages the proliferator progressed, the easier it would be to detect the activity; on the other hand, the earlier the activity could be detected, the less likely it would be that the effort would succeed—or even be undertaken.

The draft protocol to the BTWC is complex, but there are discernible key elements to the text being developed (13). These include mandatory declarations of the most relevant facilities where illegal activities might be pursued. Then there are infrequent visits and clarification procedures designed to ensure that declarations are accurate and that any ambiguities, uncertainties, or omissions in declarations are properly addressed. Additionally, there would be a system of noncompliance investigations, in cases where there was a well-founded concern, to determine whether noncompliant activity was being undertaken. The similarities of the system to that of the CWC—particularly the three-pillar regime elements of declarations, visits, and noncompliance investigations—are obvious. Nevertheless, there are also differences. It is much more difficult, for example, to see how quantitative limits on production could be agreed and monitored effectively. In the main, chemical warfare agents have to be made from specific precursors and produced and stockpiled in large quantities, whereas biological agents can be produced from small quantities of seed stocks very rapidly. Moreover, to produce large quantities of dangerous chemical warfare agents, a large site with special safety characteristics would be needed, whereas many commercial sites would have fermentation capabilities adequate for producing biological weapons.

Despite such difficulties, the Ad Hoc Group has made considerable progress. What is of interest here is that though determination of the most relevant facilities (that is, those that will have to be declared and visited) will depend on a number of characteristics, the type of agents being used is one of the critical factors. The AHG has spent much time, therefore, discussing the criteria that should be used and the agents that will be listed. Although the eventual list will only be illustrative of what the General Purpose Criterion prohibits, it will be helpful in understanding the agents of most concern to state parties.

LIST OF AGENTS

After each negotiating session the latest version of the "rolling text" of the verification protocol is published (14). This contains a statement on the criteria for selection of agents and the list of agents being considered. More usefully, from our point of view, the state parties have produced numerous working papers with more details of the reasoning behind their own input to these discussions. Among the most recent of these working papers is a detailed review "Evaluation of Biological Agents and Toxins" by the Republic of Croatia. This paper deals with twenty-four toxins and bioregulators.

The paper includes two tables of data relevant to these agents. In the first, it applies a set of criteria that are used for human pathogens. Table 9.1 is an extract of data for six examples from this table. The first column has a plus sign if the example is known to have been weaponized. No information is given as to the basis of the assessment that twelve toxins have been weaponized, and the working paper states that it is not 100 percent certain of whether such weaponization has occurred in every case. The remaining columns indicate a plus sign for a dangerous property and a negative sign for a less dangerous one. The final column totals up both plus and minus signs for the row of data for each toxin/bioregulator example. So the higher the total number of plus signs, the more dangerous the agent.

The second table in the Croatian paper gives additional data for toxins and bioregulators. An extract for the same examples used in Table 9.1 is given in Table 9.2. Here low numbers in the columns indicate the most dangerous contingency. Therefore, in the first column, "Toxicity," a figure

Table 9.1 Toxin Assessment According to Criteria for Selecting Toxins as Toxin Weapons

Toxin/ Bioregulator	Weaponized	High Toxicity	High Morbidity	Intoxication by Variety of Routes— Respiratory Route	High Level of Incapacity/ Mortality	No Effective Prophylaxis/ Therapy	Stability in the Environment	Difficulty of Detection/ Identification	Ease of Production	Totals +/−
Aflatoxins	+	−	+	+	+	+	+	+	+	8/1
Botulinum toxins	+	+	+	+	+	−	+	+	+	8/1
Ricin	+	+	+	+	+	+	+	+	+	9/0
Saxitoxin	+	+	+	+	+	+	+	+	−	8/1
Staphylococcal enterotoxins (SEB)	+	+	+	+	+	+	+	+	+	9/0
Endothelin/sarafotoxin	−	+	+	+	+	+	+	+	+	8/1

Source: From reference 15.

Table 9.2 Toxin Risk Assessment

Toxin/ Bioregulator	Toxicity	Onset	Level of Incapacity/ Mortality	Likely Methods of Dissemination	Stability in the Environment/ Storage	Ease of Decontamination	Ease of Production	Totals
Aflatoxins	7	8	5	5	5	1	3	34
Botulinum toxins	1	3	7	3	2	6	1	23
Ricin	3	6	8	3	2	5	1	28
Saxitoxin	3	2	8	3	3	7	5	31
Staphylococcal enterotoxins (SEB)	4	6	2	2	3	5	2	24
Endothelin/sarafotoxin	6	1	7	2	3	5	4	28

Source: From reference 15.

1 indicates an LD_{50} in the 10^{-9} grams/kilogram range, and a figure 10 an LD_{50} in the 10^{-3} grams/kilogram range. Similarly a figure 1 in the "Onset" column indicates an effect in minutes to hours, and a figure 10 multiple hours or days. In the column "Likely Methods of Dissemination," a figure 1 indicates that aerosolization is possible, and a figure 10 that it is not. Thus, a low figure in the final column indicates a dangerous example. These tables contain much information of interest, for example, demonstrating how similar the incapacitating capabilities of endothelin are to those of SEB.

Calculations of the number of facilities worldwide that would have to be declared, should a verification protocol be agreed, are surprisingly low (16). Selection criteria involving, for example, listed agents and high containment capabilities (required for work with dangerous agents in many countries today) lead to totals of some tens of facilities per country in many developed European states and maybe hundreds in countries like the United States. Worldwide, the total facilities to be declared, and thus subject to nonchallenge visits, are thought to number no more that 2,000 to 3,000. Moreover, because the BTWC organization will probably be smaller than the CWC organization, it is likely that it will make no more than about 100 visits in any one year. So the number of declared sites will be low and the number subject to a visit to check the declaration even smaller. Although there will be a random element in the selection of facilities to be visited, there will be a strict (low-number) limit on visits to facilities in any one state party in any one year. It obviously has to be asked whether such an arrangement is sufficient to achieve the central objectives of the mandate given to the Ad Hoc Group.

VERIFICATION OF THE BTWC

If we consider the process by which a militarily significant biological weapons capability would be acquired, the first place where its detection might be a realistic possibility is at stage four, when production is undertaken. Thus, in consideration of what facilities should be declared, those working with listed agents and having capabilities for production would seem very important.

Other triggers for the necessity of declarations would include military biological defense programs and facilities. However, we will concentrate here on the probable consequences of the triggering of declarations for a small number of major production facilities in a country that is considering undertaking an illicit, offensive, biological weapons program. We know from the program in the former Soviet Union that one easy way for a proliferator to proceed is to use the cover of a large, seemingly civil program to disguise what is being done. That was the purpose of the Biopreparat program. But if such production sites using listed agents have to be declared, a potential proliferator faces a dilemma. To declare a facility is to risk its *illegal activities* being discovered in the declaration-checking visits, but not to declare such a facility requires that *the facility itself and its illegal activities are totally concealed* from the outside world. If it is discovered, it will be potentially open to challenge investigation and, again, discovery of its true purpose. This is a more sophisticated view of what verification is really about and is well understood by professional members of the intelligence community (17). An appropriate analogy would be the use of random checks of a small proportion of submitted returns (declarations) by the income tax authorities in some countries. A man may wish to cheat on his tax declarations but if he decides to take the risk, he must bear in mind that a random routine check could lead to a stringent and comprehensive investigation. The overall result, both for an income tax cheat and a potential proliferator, is a mass of verification consequences for a comparatively small degree of checking.

A look at the work of the United Nations Special Commission in Iraq shows just how successful a system of declarations and checking can be, even in the face of years of determined efforts to hide an offensive program (18). The special commission's seven-year investigation of the Iraqi biological weapons program covered three distinct periods. During the first period, it sought to resolve concerns about a possible program. Iraq strongly denied that it ever had such a program. In the second period, the special commission concentrated on developing a system to monitor Iraqi facilities and industry. Only in 1994, in the third period, did the special commission return to the question of the biological weapons program. The special commission had more extensive powers than would be agreed in a normal multilateral disarmament treaty; Iraq also had years in which to cover its tracks. Thus, the UNSCOM inspectors' task was far from straightforward.

We can gain an insight into the kind of concerns that governments had at the start of UNSCOM's activities from a document produced for the Canadian External Affairs and International Trade department in 1991 (19). The document's title was *Collateral Analysis and Verification of Biological and Toxin Research in Iraq.* A search of various open databases revealed 10,000 publications from Iraq in the period 1969–1991. A set of key words was then used to narrow these down to 991 publications, which formed the basis of the analysis. The investigators were able to conclude that a major trend could be detected in Iraqi biological research originating from many different laboratories. Initially, there was a low level of activity, then a major increase in 1979–1981, a decrease in 1983–1985, and then another major increase. The Canadian study notes that there will always be a significant time lag between the decision to increase funding in any area of research and the eventual research output, and so the increased publications first observed around 1979 may reflect a shift in research priorities decided upon around 1975 (19). That would appear to fit with what we now know of the initiation of the Iraqi program in the 1970s and the failure of its first efforts.

More specifically, the study notes that what is *not* found in the open literature is often also of great significance. The following statement is revealing: "*Bacillus anthracis* (the bacterium which causes anthrax) and *Clostridium botulinum* (the source of botulinum neurotoxin which causes botulism) were *each* the subject of only one publication over the period 1969–1991. In the case of anthrax, this is surprising because it is a potential health hazard in the region." As we now know, both were weaponized by Iraq in the 1980s and early 1990s. Of particular interest is the way in which the Canadians whittled down the initial set of 10,000 Iraqi publications to those of interest by using a series of key words. The study's section on methodology states:

> Search strategies were used to identify Iraqi research associated with the following topics:
>
> Microbiology, virology, bacteriology, infectious diseases;
> toxins, neurotoxins . . . ;
> recombinant DNA, gene-cloning;
> large-scale production, fermentation, bioreactors;
> vaccine technology, immunology, immunization;
> aerosol, lyophilization;
> specific biological agents . . . ;
> bioregulators. . . . (19)

The study states that the presence of these key words does not necessarily imply any direct connection between the published work and a biological weapons program, but "[t]hese key words are indicators that are considered to have a potential relationship to biological warfare research" (19). The specific key words used for toxins, biological agents, and bioregulators are listed in separate tables of the study; those for toxins and bioregulators are reproduced here:

Toxin Key Words

abrin	bungarotoxin	mycotoxin	saxitoxin
apamin	conotoxin	palytoxin	tetanus toxin
brevetoxin	curare	phospholipase	tetrodotoxin
batrachotoxin	diamphotoxin	ricin	tubocurare
botulinum toxin	latrotoxin	sarafotoxin	

Bioregulator Key Words

angiotensin	delta sleep–inducing	gastrin	Substance P
atrial natriuretic	peptide	gonadoliberin	thyroliberin
peptide	dynorphin	neurotensin	vasopressin (19)
bombesin	endorphin	neuropeptide Y	
bradykinin	endothelin	somatostatin	
cholecystokinin	enkephalin		

The substances we have discussed in detail are included on these lists, as indeed are many other potential agents. In the detailed analysis of research output, it is noted, for instance, in regard to one Iraqi institute, that "[a] topic of research that stands out is a series of papers examining the nasal absorption of the bioregulator enkephalin" (19). Little wonder, in retrospect, that many experts were not convinced by initial Iraqi denials of a biological weapons program.

During 1994, UNSCOM inspectors returned to the question of such a program in earnest and began to marshal their evidence and arguments in an effort to prove what had long been suspected. By April 1995 the inspectors had no definitive proof, but they did have three pieces of evidence that strongly suggested that production of biological weapons had been undertaken by Iraq. The first piece of evidence concerned thirty-nine tons of complex growth material for microorganisms that had been imported. Iraq said this was for use in hospitals for disease diagnosis, but hospitals generally use only small quantities of such material and buy it in small packages to avoid waste. Iraq bought its material in bulk in large drums. Furthermore, the material was not ideally suited for hospital diagnostic work, but it was just right for the large-scale production of biological materials. Finally, Iraq was unable to explain convincingly the fate of seventeen tons of this material.

The second piece of evidence was the biological production facility at Al Hakem. This was said to be a single-cell protein, animal feed factory, but its remote setting, level of security, and superfluous design features did not fit that story. Third and finally, Iraq had purchased items such as four filling machines and a spray dryer that could produce one to ten micron-sized particles. It had also attempted to obtain particularly virulent strains of biological agents. By April 1995, therefore, the special commission reported its assessment to the United Nations Security Council "that Iraq obtained or sought to obtain all the items and materials required to produce biological warfare agents in Iraq. With Iraq's failure to account for all these items and materials for legitimate purposes, the only conclusion that can be drawn is that there is a high risk that they were purchased and in part used for proscribed purposes—the production of agents for biological weapons" (18).

It is important to stress that this conclusion came about through Iraq making declarations of its activities and inspectors attempting to validate these declarations. Although there was no one piece of evidence that un-equivocally pointed to the UNSCOM conclusion, the different pieces of the jigsaw would only fit if interpreted in that way. After 1995 the process of Iraqi declarations and their checking by the inspectorate continued. The stalemate at the end of the 1990s resulted from the fact that Iraq had still not been able to convince international experts that it was telling the truth and that the full scope of its activities had been revealed. It has been ar-gued that, to convince international experts, Iraq will need to provide a "truly full, final, and complete disclosure of its biological weapons activi-ties" (19); support this with data and evidence; and facilitate the verifica-tion of its full final and complete account. In short, as one insider con-cluded: "Some have suggested that the goal of designing a BW verifications mechanism, which can detect noncompliance, is unattainable. The Special Commission has proven that it is not impossible to detect a concealed BW program, even when it is carefully hidden" (18). Yet even if it is possible to strengthen the BTWC along these lines, and the strengthened convention provides an effective mechanism to detect cheating, is that all that can or should be done?

THE WEB OF DETERRENCE

We have concentrated here on the central verification requirements set out in the mandate given to the present Ad Hoc Group. Even in the mandate, however, there is a requirement for specific measures to ensure effective and full implementation of Article X of the Biological and Toxin Weapons Convention *itself*. Article X is concerned with cooperation and peaceful development, and its implementation is part of the bargain necessary to achieve a high level of participation in a strengthened convention. That, surely, is a price worth paying, for it must be to universal advantage that the 141 state parties to the BTWC are also bound by the verification pro-tocol. In the future, also, we would all benefit if states that have not yet joined the BTWC were to become state parties to a newly strengthened regime. Though Article X may appear out of place in an arms control agreement, it must be remembered that for many countries their primary problems lie in controlling natural disease outbreaks and not with the pos-sibility of biological warfare. Thus cooperation in some appropriate as-pects of modern biotechnology would provide a strong inducement for them to join the regime (20).

In deciding to set up the current Ad Hoc Group, the 1994 special confer-ence stated that it was determined to strengthen the effectiveness and improve the implementation of the convention (21). The Ad Hoc Group's remit thus ex-tends beyond just verification measures and Article X measures. It should also be concerned with the enactment of the effective national legislation that will be required to bring the strengthened convention into force. Such legislation will also help greatly in the prevention of bioterrorism. As with the CWC, it will be the responsibility of state parties to ensure that all the potential agents *not* listed in the international agreement are only used for peaceful purposes. The Ad Hoc Group will also have to concern itself with the eventual implementation of a more effective and acceptable system of export controls for sensitive materials and equipment, in order to make the kind of proliferation embarked upon by Iraq more difficult. Such developments would contribute toward what has been called a "web of deterrence" against biological weapons programs (22). While centered appropriately on comprehensive and verifiable global arms control agreements, this web would also include broad export controls and effective defensive measures to reduce the perceived utility of biological weapons. Finally, an effective web of deterrence would impose a commitment upon the international community to respond effectively to transgression of the norm of nonuse of these weapons, embodied in the 1925 Geneva Protocol and the BTWC.

The Web of Deterrence

- Comprehensive, verifiable, and global CB arms control to create a risk of detection and a climate of political unacceptability for CB weapons;
- Broad export monitoring and controls to make it difficult and expensive for a proliferator to obtain necessary materials;
- Effective CB defensive and protective measures to reduce the military utility of CB weapons; and
- A range of determined and effective national and international responses to CB acquisition and/or use. (22)

RESERVATIONS

It would be misleading to give the impression that the BTWC will *necessarily* soon be strengthened by an effective verification protocol, and that this will form the basis for a long-term web of deterrence to prevent the proliferation of offensive biological warfare programs. To begin with, the worldwide chemical industry—including that in the United States—strongly supported the negotiation of the CWC, but there were, nevertheless, important reservations placed on the implementation of the convention during its ratification in the U.S. Senate. Unfortunately, the powerful U.S. biotechnology industry has adopted the position that the nonchallenge visits element of a three-pillar verification protocol to the BTWC should be opposed, because visits could allegedly put important commercial proprietary information at risk (23). This must necessarily reduce the chances of an effective protocol being ratified by the U.S. Senate, even if it can be agreed internationally.

The message from any such unilateral enactment of reservations will surely not be lost on other states that, for different reasons, might be less than enthusiastic about seeing an effective BTWC verification protocol in place.

So it is possible that for some time yet there will be no effective constraint on the proliferation of offensive biological weapons programs. We have concentrated on the problems that may be caused by the rapid developments under way in biotechnology and genomics, but there are other factors that need to be taken into account. It is difficult to know, from the information available, just how many offensive biological weapons programs are in existence or in what stages of development they are. It seems probable that there are biological weapons programs in various stages of development, and they appear to be concentrated in regions of instability and potential conflict (24). In this situation, without an effective BTWC, there is an ever-present possibility that misperceptions about the activities of other states will lead to the initiation or acceleration of offensive biological weapons programs. There is no reason to believe that these weapon systems are exempt from this standard security dilemma. If there are even *nascent* offensive programs in existence, the conversion of hostility into open conflict is likely to accelerate their development, given the promise of great offensive benefits or deterrence capabilities (25). Given also the wide range of ways in which a proliferator might proceed, it is difficult to predict where an arms race involving biological weapons might end, after years of large-scale funding and the pressures generated by significant threats to nations' security.

The immediate priority must, of course, be to achieve both the strengthening of the BTWC through a verification protocol and its widest possible acceptance in the first decade of the twenty-first century. It must be stressed, however, that we are presently in the very early stages of a revolution in the life sciences. The revolution in bacteriology initiated by people like Louis Pasteur and Robert Koch in the final decades of the nineteenth century had profound effects for the good of humankind throughout the twentieth. It has also led to the development of a series of increasingly sophisticated, scientifically based, offensive biological warfare programs (4). Constraining the further development of such programs in the first few decades of the twenty-first century will probably require more than just strengthening of the BTWC. It is to such wider issues of arms control and beyond that we return in the final chapter.

REFERENCES

1. M. R. Dando (1999). The development of international legal constraints on biological warfare in the 20th century. In M. Kaskenniemi et al., eds., *The Finnish Yearbook of International Law*. Vol. 8. The Hague: Martinus Nijhoff, pp. 1–69.

2. A. Boserup (1973). *CBW and the Law of War*. Vol. 3 of *The Problem of Chemical and Biological Warfare*. Stockholm: Almqvist and Wiksell (for SIPRI).

3. M. R. Dando (1996). *Biological Warfare in the 21st Century*. London: Brassey's.

4. V. Nathanson, M. Darvell, and M. R. Dando (1999). *Biotechnology, Weapons and Humanity*. London: Harwood Academic (for the British Medical Association).

5. Operations Research Group (1961). *Arms Control of CBR Weapons. I. Military Aspects*. U.S. Army Chemical Corps, Army Chemical Center, Maryland, 9 February.

6. J. B. Tucker (1994). Dilemmas of a dual-use technology: Toxins in medicine and warfare. *Politics and the Life Sciences* 13, no. 1: 51–62.

7. M. R. Dando (1998). An arms control regime for the 21st century. In T. Woodhouse et al., eds., *Peacekeeping and Peacemaking: Towards Effective Intervention in Post–Cold War Conflicts*. London: Macmillan, pp. 103–130.

8. J. B. Tucker (1998). Verification provisions of the Chemical Weapons Convention and their relevance to the Biological Weapons Convention. In A. E. Smithson, ed., *Biological Weapons Proliferation: Reasons for Concern: Courses of Action*. Washington, D.C.: The Henry L. Stimson Center, pp. 77–106.

9. T. Pfeiffer (1999). The CWC at the two-year mark: An interview with Dr. John Gee. *Arms Control Today* (April/May): 3–9.

10. A. E. Smithson (1999). Tall order: Crafting a meaningful verification protocol for the Biological Weapons Convention. In S. Wright, ed., *Current Problems of Biological Warfare and Disarmament*. Preprint of a symposium, UNIDIR, Geneva, pp. 38–48.

11. R. A. Zilinskas (1986). Verification of the Biological Weapons Convention. In E. Geissler, ed., *Biological and Toxin Weapons Today*. Oxford: Oxford University Press (for SIPRI), pp. 82–107.

12. Office of Technology Assessment (1993). *Technologies Underlying Weapons of Mass Destruction*. OTA-BP-ISC-115, December. United States Congress, Washington, D.C.

13. S. Pullinger (1999). *Preventing Deliberate Disease: The Emerging Verification Protocol*. London: International Security Information Service, Centre for Defence Studies, Kings College.

14. United Nations (1999). *Procedural Report of the Ad Hoc Group of the States Parties to the Convention on the Prohibition of the Development, Production and Stockpiling of Bacteriological (Biological) and Toxin Weapons and on Their Destruction*. BWC/AD HOC GROUP/45 (Part 1), Geneva, 4 April.

15. Republic of Croatia (1999). *Evaluation of Biological Agents and Toxins*. BWC/AD HOC GROUP/WP.356/Rev. 1, Geneva, 19 July.

16. G. S. Pearson (1998). *The Strengthened BTWC Protocol: An Integrated Regime*. Briefing Paper No. 10. Department of Peace Studies, University of Bradford.

17. D. J. MacEachin (1998). Routine and challenge: Two pillars of verification. *CBW Conventions Bulletin* 39: 1–3.

18. S. Black (1999). UNSCOM and the Iraqi biological weapons program: Implications for arms control. In S. Wright, ed., *Current Problems of Biological Warfare and Disarmament*. Preprint of a symposium, UNIDIR, Geneva, pp. 13–25.

19. Canada (1991). *Collateral Analysis and Verification of Biological and Toxin Research in Iraq*. Ministry of External Affairs and International Trade, Ottawa.

20. G. S. Pearson (1999). *Article VII Measures: Optimizing the Benefits*. Briefing Paper No. 22. Department of Peace Studies, University of Bradford.

21. United Nations (1994). *Final Report. Special Conference of the States Parties to the Convention on the Prohibition of the Development, Production and Stockpiling of Bacteriological (Biological) and Toxin Weapons and on Their Destruction.* BWC/SPCONF/1, Geneva, 19–30 September.

22. G. S. Pearson (1993). Prospects for chemical and biological arms control: The web of deterrence. *The Washington Quarterly* (spring): 145–162.

23. M. R. Dando (1998) *The Strengthened BTWC Protocol: Implications for the Biotechnology and Pharmaceutical Industry.* Briefing Paper No. 17. Department of Peace Studies, University of Bradford.

24. Office of Technology Assessment (1993). *Proliferation of Weapons of Mass Destruction: Assessing the Risks.* OTA-ISC-559, August. United States Congress, Washington D.C.

25. J. Jelsma (1995). Military implications of biotechnology. In M. Fransman, ed., *The Biotechnology Revolution.* Oxford: Blackwell, pp. 284–297.

10

The Future of Arms Control

This book began with Stuart Croft's suggestion that the international community has developed a set of arms control tools to deal with the various problems that have arisen in different historical periods (1). Although the nature of the global order that will evolve and stabilize as the current post–Cold War, transitional era comes to a close is still the subject of intense debate, and though some commentators are rather pessimistic about what arms control may have left to contribute, the position adopted here is in line with those who pragmatically expect to see many future roles for arms control (2, 3, 4, 5, 6). In particular, while consideration will continue to be given to a variety of ways of dealing with the proliferation of weapons of mass destruction, arms control must remain central (7, 8). As the UK Ministry of Defence stated in its major review of the threat from biological and chemical weapons in mid-1999, "[t]he foundation for managing the risks is diplomatic: international pressure to agree acceptable norms of behaviour; disarmament and non-proliferation initiatives; and preventing the supply of materials needed for biological and chemical weapons programmes" (9). The question then is, What kind of arms control is likely to develop?

INTERNATIONAL HUMANITARIAN LAW (THE LAWS OF WAR)

Since the mid-nineteenth century, the prohibition of the use of weapons that cause superfluous injury or unnecessary suffering, embodied in the St. Petersburg Declaration, has influenced multilateral arms control negotiations. After extensive use of chemical weapons in World War I had led to some 1.3 million casualties and 100,000 deaths, the International Committee of the Red Cross stated: "We wish to-day to take a stand against a barbaric

153

innovation. . . . This innovation is the use of asphyxiating and poisonous gas. . . . We protest with all the force at our command against such warfare which can only be called criminal" (10). Such revulsion, of course, helped to lead to the negotiation of the 1925 Geneva Protocol. Yet the problem with such a ban on *the use* of a weapon system is that it may well not survive the pressures of all-out warfare. It was clearly much more difficult to achieve the *total prohibition* of all such weapons in the Chemical Weapons Convention, which came about only after the Cold War had ended, when, for major states, the military utility of such weapons had diminished. Similarly, it can be argued that humanitarian principles have had only a limited impact on the negotiation of an effective verification protocol for the BTWC.

Nevertheless, it is obvious that by the 1990s, a variety of factors, particularly the types of war being fought in places like Somalia and Yugoslavia and by Iraq, raised the profile of the laws of war (11). The underlying movement, illustrated best perhaps by the agreement on an international criminal court, has seen the beginnings of change from a state-based system of implementing the laws of war to one based more on the United Nations (12). Within that general context, the Ottawa Convention on the Prohibition of the Use, Stockpiling, Production and Transfer of Anti-Personnel Mines and on Their Destruction is of particular note. According to one detailed commentary: "Perhaps the most significant aspect of the Ottawa treaty . . . is that its conclusion represents the first occasion on which an arms control agreement banning an entire category of weapons has been motivated *primarily* by humanitarian concerns" (emphasis added) (10).

The unprecedented impact of thousands of innocent civilians being maimed and killed by indiscriminately spread antipersonnel mines, and the prospects of the long-term continuation of this slaughter, had produced a widespread popular view that something had to be done to halt and reverse the process.

The popular movement to achieve a ban on antipersonnel landmines is also of interest here because of the role of the International Committee of the Red Cross. Though many organizations played a role in mobilizing world opinion, the standing of the ICRC and its willingness to push for complete disarmament despite traditional unwillingness to adopt a political position, were of great importance. As we have seen, through its Superfluous Injury or Unnecessary Suffering project, the ICRC remains highly committed to thinking through how the humanitarian laws of war should be developed in order to deal with the likely opportunities for developing novel weapons based on new technologies.

Another encouraging development in this regard was the 1995 agreement of Protocol IV to the Convention on the Prohibition or Restrictions on the Use of Certain Conventional Weapons Which May Be Deemed to

Be Excessively Injurious or to Have Indiscriminate Effects. This new protocol prohibits laser-blinding weapons and is significant because it was negotiated *before* such weapons were ever used and despite the fact that the technology had advanced so far that weapons had gone into production in a number of countries (10). Instead of the usual process, whereby international law operates more slowly than weapons deployment and efforts have to be made to reverse an existing situation, here the international community was able to agree to forestall a terrifying development. Clearly, laser weapons specifically designed to blind, could—if deployed on a large scale—lead to many soldiers being irreversibly blinded. A situation analogous in some ways to the continuing impact of antipersonnel landmines was certainly possible had such weapons not been outlawed.

In the future, therefore, we can hope to see a continuing impact of humanitarian principles on arms control and disarmament. However difficult that process had been in the twentieth century, the 1990s saw significant progress. Moreover, appropriate professional organizations, which have a cumulative impact on world opinion, have a long involvement in the debates about chemical and biological weapons (13). The ICRC itself and other medical organizations are monitoring the potential development of new biological weapons with specific effects (14).

A final feature of note in the recent development of international humanitarian law, for example, with respect to war crimes in the former Yugoslavia, is the move to hold individuals responsible for their actions, whatever their rank or position. In that regard, it has been argued by some authorities that it will eventually be necessary to supplement the Chemical Weapons Convention and the strengthened Biological and Toxin Weapons Convention with a convention *criminalizing* chemical and biological weapons (15). The first article of this proposed Convention on the Prevention and Punishment of the Crime of Developing, Producing, Acquiring, Stockpiling, Retaining, Transferring or Using Biological or Chemical Weapons is set out below. It is clear from Article I.2 that it is *no defense* that a person acted in an official capacity in carrying out the prohibited activity.

Draft Convention on the Prevention and Punishment of the Crime of Developing, Producing, Acquiring, Stockpiling, Retaining, Transferring or Using Biological or Chemical Weapons

Article I

1. Any person commits an offence if that person:
   (a) orders, directs, plans or knowingly participates in the development, production, acquisition, stockpiling, retention, transfer or use of biological or chemical weapons; or
   (b) attempts to commit any offence described in sub-paragraph (a); or

(c) assists, encourages or induces, in any way, anyone to engage in the development, production, acquisition, stockpiling, retention, transfer or use of biological or chemical weapons; or

(d) threatens to use biological or chemical weapons to cause death or injury to any person in order to compel a natural or legal person, international organization or State to do or refrain from doing any act.

2. It shall not be a defence against prosecution or extradition for the above offences that a person acted in an official capacity or under the orders or instruction of a State, a superior officer, a public or private authority or any other person or for any other reason.

3. Notwithstanding the above provisions of this Article, nothing in this Convention shall be construed as prohibiting activities that are not prohibited under the Chemical Weapons Convention or the Biological Weapons Convention or that are directed toward the fulfilment of a State's obligations under such conventions and that are conducted in accordance with its provisions. (15)

THE BIOTECHNOLOGY/GENOMICS REVOLUTION

The early decades of the twenty-first century will be characterized not just by major changes to the state system but also by the continuing impact of the biotechnology/genomics revolution. Over the course of this century, the impact of this revolution will profoundly alter our whole way of life (16). Controlling the diffusion of this technology, so that it has benign rather than malign consequences, will be one of the major tasks of the century (17). This broader problem requires further consideration, but first it has to be recognized that the technology potentially has radically destabilizing consequences.

It is sobering to recall that, until the industrial revolution, practically the only toxic substances known to humans were naturally occurring toxins such as snake venom and plant extracts. However, these were very difficult to obtain in large enough quantities for military purposes (18). The situation had not greatly changed by the end of the nineteenth century, but there was a growing awareness that the developing chemical industry might be able to produce and supply much larger quantities of dangerous chemicals. In response, the international community began an attempt to prevent the development and use of such chemicals in warfare, both at the Brussels Conference of 1874 and the Hague Peace Conferences of 1899 and 1907. Unfortunately, this attempt did not prevent the development and use of chemical weapons during World War I nor the progressive discovery of more dangerous agents in midcentury. Only in the last decade of the twentieth century did an effective agreement prohibiting these weapons come into force.

The situation we face today is perhaps more complex than at the end of the nineteenth century because there are at least three emerging technologies—information technology, nanotechnology, and biotechnology—that may have major consequences (19). Progress is already rapid in each of these areas, and there is a clear indication that developments of unexpected kinds may arise from interactions between them. Concern about the rapid nature of developments in biotechnology dates from the 1980s, as do anxieties about whether such developments are covered by the Biological and Toxin Weapons Convention (20).

The implications of the ongoing revolution in biotechnology were the subject of a careful and alarming review by Matthew Meselson of Harvard University at the beginning of 1999 (21). Meselson, who has long been concerned about the proliferation of chemical and biological weapons, quoted from a prize-winning essay by a naval officer published a decade earlier by the U.S. *Naval War College Review:* "The outlook for biological weapons is grimly interesting. Weaponeers have only just begun to explore the potential of the biotechnological revolution. It is sobering to realize that far more development lies ahead than behind" (22). Meselson commented that if the prediction is correct, biotechnology will profoundly change the nature of biological weaponry and the context in which it will be used. He argued that as the biotechnology revolution progresses in the twenty-first century, our ability will move well beyond just the capacity to use pathogens effectively in warfare, for we will not only be able to harm life but also to manipulate "the processes of cognition, development, reproduction, and inheritance" (21). In Meselson's view, should such capabilities be widely used, the nature of human conflict would radically change: There would arise quite radical new means of violence, coercion, and subjugation that would have profound consequences for the future direction of human society and civilization.

This, then, is the measure of the challenge we face, and we will be mistaking this problem if we see it just as a matter of controlling the *current military* applications of biotechnology. The biotechnology revolution is already having profound affects on agriculture and health, and efforts are already being made to develop better international legal regimes for controlling the impact on environment and health (23, 24). So a correct analysis of the problem suggests that we have to view the development of international arms control agreements as the security aspect of a whole new set of international legal requirements; these requirements will have to be designed and implemented in the twenty-first century to help ensure that the new science and technology function for the benefit of and not to the detriment of human society and its environment.

There are certainly deep and difficult problems of security to be resolved in an unjust and asymmetric world, if we are to effectively control the proliferation of weapons of mass destruction (25). The broader challenge is how this aspect of our science and technology—the impact on the proliferation of weapons of mass destruction—is to be brought under the aegis of an emerging global regulatory government (26). In regard to security, Ambassador James Leonard, who negotiated the original BTWC for the United States, set out his vision in a recent presentation in which he reflected on the past and future developments of the Biological and Toxin Weapons Convention: "During the long, slow transition to a new system of international relations, the global and regional arms control treaties of the past 40 years will be complemented by additional treaty regimes covering the full range of conventional weapons" (27). This process, in his opinion, would lead to a transformation of political relations:

> These treaties will bring with them a matrix of verification procedures so penetrating, so ubiquitous and so intrusive, as to be unimaginable today. *Total transparency in military matters will be the norm that is steadily and inexorably approached. Military secrecy will be seen, increasingly, as an unhealthy remnant of a previous era in which national security was protected by the balance of power.* (emphasis added) (27)

What Ambassador Leonard was arguing, therefore, was for arms control to be used in a different way from even those contemplated in Croft's broad vision. Leonard argued for arms control to be used not only for the control of weaponry but also as Ivo Daalder suggested (see Chapter 1) to help foster political change. In Leonard's view, "[t]ogether, these treaties will provide a framework of norms, obligations, procedures, rules and interactions that will foster political advances" (27).

Today as we puzzle over the U.S. Senate's rejection of the Comprehensive Test Ban Treaty, and threats to the Anti-Ballistic Missile Treaty, it is difficult to know whether we can even maintain the central elements of the arms control regime developed over the past half century (28). Yet there really is no sensible alternative to Ambassador Leonard's vision. While there appears to be an impasse in arms control of weapons of mass destruction, the necessity of preventing the further proliferation of these weapons will ensure that opportunities arise for the development of new international agreements (29). The alternative is to place ourselves at the mercy of those who favor seeking security only through the continuing military application of ever more potent scientific and technological developments.

In regard to the issue of paramount concern to us here—the strengthening of the Biological and Toxin Weapons Convention—the final word must go to the International Committee of the Red Cross. In its presentation to the United Nations First Committee in October 1999, the ICRC stated:

Recent reports, including one published by the British Medical Association early this year, have highlighted the potential for abuse of remarkable and rapid advances in the fields of microbiology, genetic engineering and biotechnology. . . . The ICRC calls on States to spare no effort in concluding negotiations next year on an effective monitoring regime for the 1972 Biological [and Toxin] Weapons Convention. (30)

The reasons for this call to "spare no effort" are not difficult to understand. The main protection we will have against the use of new biological weapons is the same as in the past: the norm accepted widely in the international community that such weapons are totally unacceptable. It is the internalization of this norm into people's value systems—their self-imposed restraints on what they consider they ought and ought not to do—that, as Geoffrey Vickers cogently argued, is of paramount importance (31). We have to preserve and develop such global norms in order to build a world where law and not raw power determines the actions of states (32). Right now we have the chance to reinforce the norm of nonuse of biological weapons through strengthening the BTWC. If we fail to agree on an effective protocol at this time, the norm will not just remain in its present state; it will, in fact be significantly damaged by that failure. It will appear that this norm is not of sufficient importance for the international community to ensure its safekeeping. Other previously "unacceptable" weapons have become incorporated into the arsenals of major states in the past, and the same could become true of biological weapons. The terrible vision of the sophisticated use of deliberate disease as a mainstream weapon of war might well then become a reality in the early decades of the twenty-first century.

REFERENCES

1. S. Croft (1996). *Strategies of Arms Control: A History and Typology.* Manchester: Manchester University Press.

2. Roundtable (T. Garton Ash, F. Fukuyama, E. Luttwak, R. Cooper, E. Hobsbawm, and P. Hassner) (1999). The global order in the 21st century. *Prospect* (August/September): 50–58.

3. I. Kenyon (1998). *The Evolution of Global and Regional Arms Control Regimes.* VM Paper 2/3. Department of Politics, University of Southampton, 5 June.

4. J. P. Zanders (1999). *The Biological and Chemical Weapons Conventions: The Jurassic Parks of Disarmament?* Stockholm: SIPRI. Mimeo.

5. B. Boutros-Ghali (1992). *New Dimensions of Arms Regulation and Disarmament in the Post–Cold War Era.* United Nations, New York, 27 October.

6. B. Roberts (1997). Arms control in the emerging strategic environment. *Contemporary Security Policy* 18, no. 1: 57–82.

7. V. A. Utgoff (1997). *Nuclear Weapons and the Deterrence of Biological and Chemical Warfare*. Occasional Paper No. 36. Henry L. Stimson Center, Washington D.C., October.

8. P. Snyder (1999). Advanced systems and concepts office. *Connection* 1, no. 1 (8 January). Defense Threat Reduction Agency, Washington, D.C.

9. Ministry of Defence (1999). *Defending Against the Threat from Biological and Chemical Weapons*. London: Ministry of Defence.

10. R. J. Mathews and T. L. H. McCormack (1999). The influence of humanitarian principles in the negotiation of arms control treaties. *IRRC* [International Review of the Red Cross] (June): 331–352.

11. A. Roberts (1998). Implementation of the laws of war in late 20th century conflicts. Part I. *Security Dialogue* 29, no. 2: 137–150.

12. A. Roberts (1998). Implementation of the laws of war in late 20th century conflicts. Part II. *Security Dialogue* 29, no. 3: 265–278.

13. J. P. Perry Robinson (1998). The impact of Pugwash on the debates over chemical and biological weapons. *Annals of the New York Academy of Sciences* 866: 224–252.

14. V. Nathanson, M. Darvell, and M. R. Dando (1999). *Biotechnology, Weapons and Humanity*. London: Harwood Academic Press.

15. M. Meselson (1998). Strengthening the BWC and Criminalising Biological Weapons Under International Law. *Chemical and Biological Conventions Bulletin* (December): 1–3.

16. J. T. Rifkin (1998). *The Biotech Century: The Coming Age of Genetic Commerce*. London: Victor Gollancz.

17. M. Moodie (1995). Beyond proliferation: The challenge of technology diffusion. *The Washington Quarterly* 18, no. 2: 183–202.

18. SIPRI (1974). *The Effects of Developments in the Biological and Chemical Sciences on CW Disarmament Negotiations*. Stockholm: SIPRI.

19. T. K. Adams (1998). Radical destabilising effects of new technologies. *Parameters* (autumn): 99–111.

20. E. Geissler (1990). Coverage of new technologies in the BWC. In E. Geissler, ed., *Strengthening the BW Convention by CBMS*. Oxford: Oxford University Press.

21. M. Meselson (1999). "The problem of biological weapons." Paper presented at the 18th stated meeting of the American Academy of Arts and Sciences, Cambridge, Mass., 13 January.

22. S. Rose (1989). The coming explosion of silent weapons. *Naval War College Review* (summer): 1–21.

23. G. S. Pearson (1997). The complementary role of environmental and security biological control regimes in the 21st century. *Journal of the American Medical Association* 278, no. 5: 369–372.

24. D. P. Fidler (1997). The role of international law in the control of emerging infectious disease. *Bulletin Institut Pasteur* 95: 57–92.

25. D. Mutimur (1998). Reconstituting security? The practices of proliferation control. *European Journal of International Relations* 4, no. 1: 99–129.

26. K. Jayasuriya (1999). Globalization, law and the transformation of sovereignty: The emergence of global regulatory governance. *Indiana Journal of Global Legal Studies* 6, no. 2: 425–455.

27. J. Leonard (1997). Keynote address. The control of biological weapons: Retrospective and prospective. In J. Tucker, ed., *Inspection Procedures for Compliance Monitoring of the Biological Weapons Convention*. CGSR-97-002, December. Monterey Institute of International Studies and Center for Global Security Studies, Lawrence Livermore Laboratory, Livermore, Calif.

28. S. Pullinger (1999). *The Condition of Nuclear Arms Control.* Special Briefing, International Security Information Service, London, November.

29. J. Dhanapala (1999). Implementing Global Interests: The UN and arms control. *Arms Control Today* (September/October): 3–8.

30. International Committee of the Red Cross (1999). *Statement to the First Committee on Agenda Items 76, 80, 83.* United Nations General Assembly, 54th Session, 20 October.

31. M. R. Dando (1995). The management of international conflict. In M. Blunden and M. R. Dando, eds., *Rethinking Public Policy-Making: Questioning Assumptions, Challenging Beliefs.* London: Sage.

32. S. R. Ratner (1998). International law: The trial of global norms. *Foreign Policy* (spring): 65–80.

Acronyms & Abbreviations

kg	kilograms (10^3 grams)
mg	milligram (10^{-3} grams)
µg	microgram (10^{-6} grams)
ng	nanogram (10^{-9} grams)

ABM	Anti-Ballistic Missile System (Treaty)
Agent A	botulinum toxin (Iraq) (agent)
Agent C	aflatoxin (Iraq) (agent)
AHG	Ad Hoc Group of state parties to the BTWC
AIDS	acquired immune deficiency syndrome
BN	bombesin (peptide)
BTWC	Biological and Toxin Weapons Convention
BTX	botulinum toxin
BW	biological weapons (agent)
BZ	3-quinuclidinyl benzilate (nonlethal chemical agent, United States)
CB	chemical/biological
CCK	cholecystokinin
CF	cystic fibrosis
CHF	chronic heart failure
CNS	central nervous system
COU(s)	Concept(s) of Use
CRH	corticotrophic releasing hormone
CW	chemical weapons (agent)
CWC	Chemical Weapons Convention
DM	diphenylaminearsine (sternator)
DNA	deoxyribonucleic acid
DND	Department of National Defence (Canada)
DPI	dry powder inhalation (aerosol)

ET_A	endothelin receptor type A
ET_B	endothelin receptor type B
ET(s)	endothelin(s)
ET-1	endothelin-1
ET-2	endothelin-2
ET-3	endothelin-3
GPCR	G protein–coupled receptor
HGP	Human Genome Project
HIV	human immunodeficiency virus
ICRC	International Committee of the Red Cross
INF	Intermediate Nuclear Forces (Treaty)
KF	4-fluorophenoxyacetic acid (herbicide agent)
LD_{50}	dose that will kill 50 percent of the exposed population
LHRH	luteinizing hormone releasing hormone (see also LRF)
LRF	gonadoliberin (peptide; also called LRH or LHRH, luteinizing hormone releasing hormone)
LRH	luteinizing hormone releasing hormone (see also LRF)
MDI	metered dose inhalation (aerosol)
MHC II	major histocompatibility complex class II (cell)
NKA	neurokinin A
NKB	neurokinin B
NK_1	neurokinin receptor type 1
NK_2	neurokinin receptor type 2
NK_3	neurokinin receptor type 3
NPT	Nuclear Non-Proliferation Treaty
NPY	neuropeptide Y
NT	neurotensin
OPCW	Organization for the Prohibition of Chemical Weapons
PG	staphylococcal enterotoxin B (United States) (agent)
PPT-A	Substance P/neurokinin A gene
PPT-B	neurokinin B gene
PTBT	Partial Test Ban Treaty
RMA	revolution in military affairs
RNA	ribonucleic acid
SALT I	Interim Agreement on Limitation of Strategic Offensive Arms
SEB	staphylococcal enterotoxin B
SIPRI	Stockholm International Peace Research Institute
SIrUS	Superfluous Injury or Unnecessary Suffering (project)
SNP(s)	single nucleotide polymorphism(s)
SP	Substance P (peptide)
SS	somatostatin (peptide)
T-2	trichothecene (fungal mycotoxin)
TCR	T cell receptor

TRF	thyroliberin (peptide; also called TRH, thyrotrophic hormone releasing hormone)
TRH	thyrotrophic hormone releasing hormone (peptide; also called TRF, thyroliberin)
2,4-D	dichlorophenoxyacetic acid (herbicide)
2,4,5-T	trichlorophenoxyacetic acid (herbicide)
UNIDR	United Nations Institute for Disarmament Research
UNESCO	United Nations Educational, Scientific, and Cultural Organization
UNSCOM	United Nations Special Commission
VEE	Venezuelan equine encephalitis
VEREX	verification experts (meetings)
VX	nerve gas (lethal chemical agent)
XR	code name for botulinum toxin agent (United States)

Further Reading

Alibek, K., and S. Handeman (1999). *Biohazard*. New York: Random House.

Brown, T. A. (1999). *Genomes*. Oxford: BIOS Scientific Publishers.

Canada (1991). *Novel Toxins and Bioregulators: The Emerging Scientific and Technological Issues Relating to Verification and the Biological and Toxin Weapons Convention*. Ottawa, September.

Cecil, P. F. (1986). *Herbicidal Warfare: The RANCH HAND Project in Vietnam*. New York: Praeger.

Croft, S. (1996). *Strategies of Arms Control: A History and Typology*. Manchester: Manchester University Press.

Dando, M. R. (1994). *Biological Warfare in the 21st Century: Biotechnology and the Proliferation of Biological Weapons*. London: Brassey's.

———. (1996). *A New Form of Warfare: The Rise of Non-Lethal Weapons*. London: Brassey's.

———. (1999). The impact of the development of modern biology and medicine on the evolution of offensive biological warfare programs in the twentieth century. *Defense Analysis* 15, no. 1: 43–62.

Franz, D. (1997). Clinical recognition and management of patients exposed to biological warfare agents. *Journal of the American Medical Association* 278, no. 5: 399–411.

Hamilton, M. G. (1998). Toxins: The emerging threat. *ASA Newsletter* 98, no. 3: 1, 20–25.

Lander, E. S. (1996). The new genomics: Global views of biology. *Science* (274): 536–539.

Office of Technology Assessment (1993). *Technologies Underlying Weapons of Mass Destruction*. OTA-BP-ISC-115, December. United States Congress, Washington, D.C.

Perry Robinson, J. (1991). *The Rise of CB Weapons*. Vol. 1 of *The Problem of Chemical and Biological Warfare*. Stockholm: Almqvist and Wiksell (for SIPRI).

Porter, R. (1997). *The Greatest Benefit to Mankind: A Medical History of Humanity from Antiquity to the Present*. London: HarperCollins.

Rifkin, J. T. (1998). *The Biotech Century: The Coming Age of Genetic Commerce*. London: Victor Gollancz.

Rogers, P., and Dando, M. R. (1992). *A Violent Peace: Global Security After the Cold War*. London: Brassey's.

167

Rogers, P., Whitby, S., and Dando, M. R. (1999). Biological warfare against crops. *Scientific American* (June): 70–75.

Roundtable (1999). The global order in the 21st century. *Prospect* (August/September): 50–58.

Stahl, S. M. (1996). *Essential Psychopharmacology: Neuroscientific Basis and Clinical Applications.* Cambridge: Cambridge University Press.

United Nations (1970). *Chemical and Bacteriological (Biological) Weapons and the Effects of Their Possible Use.* New York.

World Health Organization (1970). *Health Aspects of Chemical and Biological Weapons.* Geneva.

Zilinskas, Raymond A., ed. (2000). *Biological Warfare: Modern Offense and Defense.* Boulder, Colo.: Lynne Rienner Publishers.

Index

abrin, 21, 47, 49, 146
Abrus precatorius (jequirity bean), 47
acetylcholine, 30, 56, 74, 75, 76, 92
acetylcholinesterase, 30
acquired immune deficiency syndrome
   (AIDS) 60, 119
adenovirus(es), 129
Ad Hoc Group (BTWC), 135, 141,
   144, 148, 149; mandate, 136
aerobiology, 104, 105, 108, 136
aerosol(s): attack 51, 108; behavior in
   lung, 108; delivery 40, 110;
   environmental stability, 41;
   infection, 106, 136; inhalation,
   73–75, 83, 95, 109; Iraqi research,
   146; respirable, 51, 54; stability, 41;
   vaccination, 106
aflatoxin(s), 117; as biological weapons
   agent, 22, 48, 117; bombs, 117; as
   "ethnic" weapon, 22, 125
African bees, 47
agent 2,4-D, 25–27, 123
agent 2,4,5-T, 25, 27, 123
Agent 15, 117, 118
Agent Blue, 25
Agent BZ, 30, 118
Agent KF (4-fluorophenoxyacetic
   acid), 123
Agent Orange, 25; use in Vietnam, 27
Agent XR, 21
agricultural warfare, 123
Alibek, Ken, 59, 83, 105, 108, 110, 119
alkaloids, 47
American Association for the Advancement of Science (AAAS), 33

amino acids, 53, 55, 70, 74, 80, 81, 91,
   92
anthrax, 11, 18, 104, 120, 146; aerosol
   delivery to lungs, 110; as biological
   weapons agent, 11, 18, 22, 34, 41,
   59; industrial inhalation, 106;
   weapons-grade agents, 108, 117,
   120
Anti-Ballistic Missile System Treaty
   (ABM; 1972), 3, 5, 158
antibiotic resistance, 41; of plague, 11
antibody: -enzyme complex, 112; in
   humoral immunity, 61; monoclonal,
   21, 112; proteins, 21; -receptor sites,
   21; response, 48, specific, 37; -toxin
   chimeric molecules, 21, 112
antigen(s), 61
antipersonnel: agents, 17, 19; mine(s),
   9, 10, 89, 154, 155; munition(s), 19
antiplant/crop agents, 19, 24–26, 27
antitoxin, 19, 20
arms: limitation, 4; race, 3, 99;
   regulation, 4, 6
arms control, 2–11, 150, 155;
   agreements, 139, 149, 154, 157, 158;
   and bacterial toxins, 53, 54; and
   biological weapons, 134, 149; and
   biotechnology revolution, 11; and
   chemical weapons, 134, 139, 149;
   coercive, 4, 6; Cold War conception,
   10; competitive, 3, 6, 7; and
   conventional weapons, 139, 158;
   cooperative, 3, 6, 7; international,
   10, 30; and League of Nations, 6;
   and nuclear weapons, 139; and

About the Book

Current revolutions in biotechnology and neuroscience are changing military technologies, necessitating dramatic re-evaluations in arms regulatory regimes. This book assesses how these new technologies can be used in weapons systems—by governments and terrorists alike—and whether this frightening development can be brought under effective international control.

Dando begins by surveying the existing (and arguably inadequate) control mechanisms for chemical and biological weapons. He then discusses how earlier generations of toxin and bioregulatory weapons have been developed by such states as Iraq, the former Soviet Union, and the United States, and explains, in nontechnical terms, the scientific advances that have implications for new weapons technology.

Considering how international law might be applied to constrain undesirable military developments without restricting technological developments for peaceful purposes, Dando concludes with a proposal for an integrated control regime that would link international agreements, national legislation, and trade regulations.

Malcolm Dando is professor of international security in the Department of Peace Studies, University of Bradford (UK). Trained originally as a biologist, since 1979 he has concentrated on problems of arms control and disarmament. His recent publications include *A New Form of Warfare* and *Peacekeeping and Peacemaking* (coauthored with T. Woodhouse and R. Bruce).